180 DAYS™
of
Reading
for Seventh Grade

As You Read

Underline information that is new or interesting.
Put a star next to information you already knew.

The Ties That Bind Dogs and Wolves

Even if you don't have a pet dog, you probably know that they often love to roll around in foul-smelling stuff. This could be mud, a dead animal, poop, garbage, or even places where these things used to be but aren't anymore. This "upside-down dance" includes dogs rubbing their necks, faces, sides, and backs, for a while...unless they're interrupted by their owners. But what meaning or purpose fuels this unusual behavior?

Researchers believe this behavior is a reminder that dogs came from wild wolves. Wolves roll in stinky stuff to communicate to their pack back at home that they have found a potential food source. Imagine that a lone wolf finds a deer carcass, and she rolls around in it, bathing herself in its scent. Then, she goes back to her pack, who instantly recognize the scent. They then know to follow the stinky wolf to their next meal. This behavior is just one example of dog behavior being similar to wolves.

A dog (top) and a wolf (bottom) roll on their backs.

another similarity between dogs and is how they communicate vocally gh barking, growling, whining, yelping, whimpering, and howling. Dogs make these noises for lots of reasons, and some dogs make them more than others. A dog will bark when it is hungry, tir happy, angry, uncomfortable, excited, and more. Overall, dogs bark a lot more do. Wolves reserve barking for special circumstances, such as to express fear or alarm le, a mother wolf who sees a pup near a dangerous riverbank might bark to get on.

y of a dog's behaviors have their roots in wolf behaviors. Does your dog art their squeaky toys? Think about what a wolf might do when it catc Does your dog love to jump up and down onto you? Consider that w the corner of adult wolves' mouths, triggering the adults to regurgitat o eat. Does your dog love to chase cars, mail carriers, squirrels, or r sponding to their ancient need to hunt, even if they don't plan on ac g or anyone. When you consider these deeply rooted behaviors, y g is indeed a wild wolf!

Authors

Joe Rhatigan

Monika Davies

Jennifer Edgerton, Ed.M.

Program Credits

Corinne Burton, M.A.Ed., *President* and *Publisher*
Emily R. Smith, M.A.Ed., *SVP of Content Development*
Véronique Bos, *VP of Creative*
Lynette Ordoñez, *Content Manager*
Ashley Oberhaus, M.Ed., *Content Specialist*
Melissa Laughlin, *Editor*
David Slayton, *Assistant Editor*
Jill Malcom, *Graphic Designer*

Standards

A division of Teacher Created Materials
5482 Argosy Avenue
Huntington Beach, CA 92649
www.tcmpub.com/shell-education
ISBN 979-8-7659-2262-0
© 2024 Shell Educational Publishing, Inc.

Table of Contents

Introduction

The Need for Practice

To be successful in today's reading classroom, students must deeply understand both concepts and procedures so that they can discuss and demonstrate their understanding. Demonstrating understanding is a process that must be continually practiced for students to be successful. According to Robert Marzano, "Practice has always been, and always will be, a necessary ingredient to learning procedural knowledge at a level at which students execute it independently" (2010, 83). Practice is especially important to help students apply reading comprehension strategies and word-study skills. *180 Days of Reading* offers teachers and parents a full page of reading comprehension and word recognition practice activities for each day of the school year.

The Science of Reading

For some people, reading comes easily. They barely remember how it happened. For others, learning to read takes more effort.

The goal of reading research is to understand the differences in how people learn to read and find the best ways to help all students learn. The term *Science of Reading* is commonly used to refer to this body of research. It helps people understand how to provide instruction in learning the code of the English language, how to develop fluency, and how to navigate challenging text and make sense of it.

Much of this research has been around for decades. In fact, in the late 1990s, Congress commissioned a review of the reading research. In 2000, the National Reading Panel (NRP) published a report that became the backbone of the Science of Reading. The NRP report highlights five components of effective reading instruction. These include the following:

- **Phonemic Awareness:** understanding and manipulating individual speech sounds
- **Phonics:** matching sounds to letters for use in reading and spelling
- **Fluency:** reading connected text accurately and smoothly
- **Vocabulary:** knowing the meanings of words in speech and in print
- **Reading Comprehension:** understanding what is read

There are two commonly referenced frameworks that build on reading research and provide a visual way for people to understand what is needed to learn to read. In the mid-1980s, a framework called the Simple View of Reading was introduced (Gough and Tunmer 1986). It shows that reading comprehension is possible when students are able to decode (or read) the words and have the language to understand the words.

The Simple View of Reading

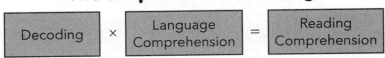

$$\text{Decoding} \times \text{Language Comprehension} = \text{Reading Comprehension}$$

Another framework that builds on the research behind the Science of Reading is Scarborough's Reading Rope (Scarborough 2001). It shows specific skills needed for both language comprehension and word recognition. The "strands" of the rope for language comprehension include having background content knowledge, knowing vocabulary, understanding language structure, having verbal reasoning, and understanding literacy. Word recognition includes phonological awareness, decoding skills, and sight recognition of familiar words (Scarborough 2001). As individual skills are strengthened and practiced, they become increasingly strategic and automatic to promote reading comprehension.

The Science of Reading (cont.)

Many parts of our understanding of how people learn to read stand the test of time and have been confirmed by more recent studies. However, new research continues to add to the understanding of reading. Some of this research shows the importance of wide reading (reading about a variety of topics), motivation, and self-regulation. The conversation will never be over, as new research will continue to refine the understanding of how people learn to read. There is always more to learn!

180 Days of Reading has been informed by this reading research. This series provides opportunities for students to practice the skills that years of research indicate contribute to reading growth. There are several features in this book that are supported by the Science of Reading.

Text Selection

- Carefully chosen texts offer experiences in a **wide range of text types**. Each unit includes nonfiction, fiction, and a nontraditional text type or genre (e.g., letters, newspaper articles, advertisements, menus).

- Texts intentionally build upon one another to help students **build background knowledge** from day to day.

- Engaging with texts on the same topic for a thematic unit enables students to become familiar with related **vocabulary**, **language structure**, and **literacy knowledge**. This allows reading to become increasingly strategic and automatic, leading to better **fluency** and **comprehension**.

Activity Design

- Specific **language comprehension** and **word-recognition skills** are reinforced throughout the activities.

- Each text includes a purpose for reading and an opportunity to practice various reading strategies through annotation. This promotes **close reading** of the text.

- Paired fiction and nonfiction texts are used to promote **comparison** and encourage students to **make connections** between texts within a unit.

- Students **write to demonstrate understanding** of the texts. Students provide written responses in a variety of forms, including short answers, open-ended responses, and creating their own versions of nontraditional texts.

This book provides the regular practice of reading skills that students need as they develop into excellent readers.

How to Use This Resource

Unit Structure Overview

This resource is organized into twelve units. Each three-week unit follows a consistent format for ease of use.

Week 1: Nonfiction

Day 1	Students read nonfiction and answer multiple-choice questions.
Day 2	Students read nonfiction and answer multiple-choice questions.
Day 3	Students read nonfiction and answer multiple-choice, short-answer, and open-response questions.
Day 4	Students read a longer nonfictional text, answer multiple-choice questions, and complete graphic organizers.
Day 5	Students reread the text from Day 4 and answer reading-response questions..

Week 2: Fiction

Day 1	Students read fiction and answer multiple-choice questions.
Day 2	Students read fiction and answer multiple-choice questions.
Day 3	Students read fiction and answer multiple-choice, short-answer, and open-response questions.
Day 4	Students read a longer fictional text, answer multiple-choice questions, and complete graphic organizers.
Day 5	Students reread the text from Day 4 and answer reading-response questions.

Week 3: Nontraditional Text

Day 1	Students read nontraditional text and answer multiple-choice and open-response questions.
Day 2	Students complete close-reading activities with paired texts from the unit.
Day 3	Students complete close-reading activities with paired texts from the unit.
Day 4	Students create their own nontraditional texts.
Day 5	Students write their own versions of the nontraditional text from Day 1.

How to Use This Resource (cont.)

Unit Structure Overview (cont.)

Paired Texts

State standards have brought into focus the importance of preparing students for college and career success by expanding their critical-thinking and analytical skills. It is no longer enough for students to read and comprehend a single text on a topic. Rather, the integration of ideas across texts is crucial for a more comprehensive understanding of themes presented by authors.

Literacy specialist Jennifer Soalt has written that paired texts are "uniquely suited to scaffolding and extending students' comprehension" (2005, 680). She identifies three ways in which paired fiction and nonfiction are particularly effective in increasing comprehension: the building of background knowledge, the development of vocabulary, and the increase in student motivation (Soalt 2005).

Each three-week unit in *180 Days of Reading* is connected by a common theme or topic. Packets of each week's or each unit's practice pages can be prepared for students.

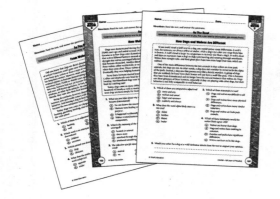

During Week 1, students read nonfictional texts and answer questions.

During Week 2, students read fictional texts and answer questions.

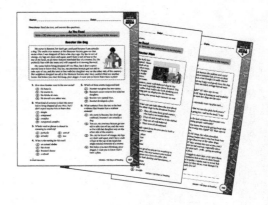

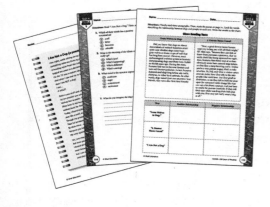

During Week 3, students read nontraditional texts (advertisements, poems, letters, etc.), answer questions, and complete close-reading and writing activities.

How to Use This Resource *(cont.)*

Student Practice Pages

Practice pages reinforce grade-level skills across a variety of reading concepts for each day of the school year. Each day's reading activity is provided as a full practice page, making them easy to prepare and implement as part of a morning routine, at the beginning of each reading lesson, or as homework.

Practice Pages for Weeks 1 and 2

Days 1 and 2 of each week follow a consistent format, with a short text passage and multiple-choice questions.

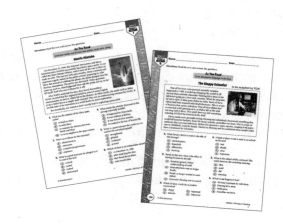

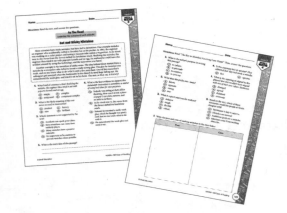

Days 3 and 4 have a combination of multiple-choice, short-answer, and open-response questions.

On day 5, students complete text-based writing prompts.

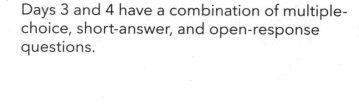

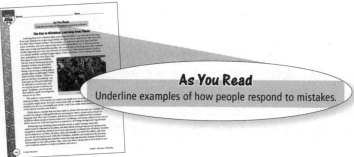

The As You Read activities give students a purpose for reading the texts and provide opportunities to practice various reading skills and strategies.

How to Use This Resource (cont.)

Student Practice Pages (cont.)
Practice Pages for Week 3

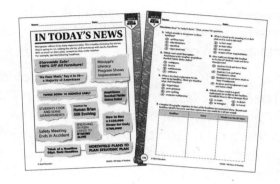

Day 1 of this week follows a consistent format, with a nontraditional text and multiple-choice and open-response questions.

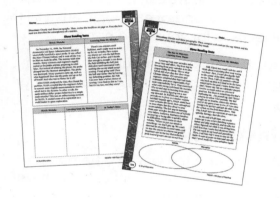

On days 2 and 3, students engage in close-reading activities of paired texts. Students are encouraged to compare and contrast different aspects of the texts they read throughout the unit.

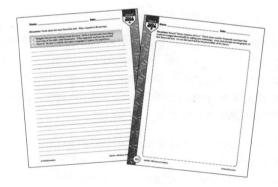

On days 4 and 5, students think about the texts in the unit, respond to a writing prompt, and construct their own versions of diverse texts. Students are encouraged to use information from texts throughout the unit to inspire and support their writing.

Instructional Options

180 Days of Reading is a flexible resource that can be used in various instructional settings for different purposes.

- Use these student pages as daily warm-up activities or as review.

- Work with students in small groups, allowing them to focus on specific skills. This setting also lends itself to partner and group discussions about the texts.

- Student pages in this resource can be completed independently during center times and as activities for early finishers.

How to Use This Resource *(cont.)*

Diagnostic Assessment

The practice pages in this book can be used as diagnostic assessments. These activity pages require students to think critically, respond to text-dependent questions, and utilize reading and writing skills and strategies. (An answer key for the practice pages is provided starting on page 230.)

For each unit, analysis sheets are provided as *Microsoft Word*® files in the digital resources. There is a *Class Analysis Sheet* and an *Individual Analysis Sheet*. Use the file that matches your assessment needs. After each week, record how many answers each student got correct on the unit's analysis sheet. Only record the answers for the multiple-choice questions. The written-response questions and graphic organizers can be evaluated using the writing rubric or other evaluation tools (see below). At the end of each unit, analyze the data on the analysis sheet to determine instructional focuses for your child or class.

The diagnostic analysis tools included in the digital resources allow for quick evaluation and ongoing monitoring of student work. See at a glance which reading genre students may need to focus on further to develop proficiency.

Using the Results to Differentiate Instruction

Once results are gathered and analyzed, use the data to inform the way to differentiate instruction. The data can help determine which concepts are the most difficult for students and that need additional instructional support and continued practice.

The results of the diagnostic analysis may show that an entire class is struggling with a particular genre. If these concepts have been taught in the past, this indicates that further instruction or reteaching is necessary. If these concepts have not been taught yet, this data is a great preassessment and demonstrates that students do not have a working knowledge of the concepts.

The results of the diagnostic analysis may also show that an individual or small group of students is struggling with a particular concept or group of concepts. Consider pulling aside these students while others are working independently to instruct further on the concept(s). You can also use the results to help identify individuals or groups of proficient students who are ready for enrichment or above-grade-level instruction. These students may benefit from independent learning contracts or more challenging activities.

Writing Rubric

A rubric for written responses is provided on page 229. Display the rubric for students to reference as they write. Score students' written responses, and provide them with feedback on their writing.

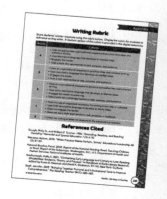

Directions: Read the text, and answer the questions.

As You Read
Underline all the things that made Coogan notable.

The First Child Star

Jackie Coogan is considered the first American child superstar. Born in 1914, Coogan started performing when he was three. He appeared in a few silent movies as well as in vaudeville. Vaudeville involved variety shows that featured comedy acts, dancing, acrobatics, music, and more. Coogan was great at mimicking other people. This got Charlie Chaplin's attention. Chaplin was a famous silent movie star. Chaplin cast seven-year-old Coogan in one of his movies. The movie was called *The Kid*, and Coogan played an orphaned child down on his luck. To this day, this movie is considered a masterpiece.

The press called Coogan "the greatest young actor in the world." Everywhere he went, he was greeted by hundreds of fans of all ages. His likeness appeared on toys, dolls, and even a brand of peanut butter. Coogan was a millionaire before he turned 10 years old!

1. Which is the best synonym for *cast* in the first paragraph?
   - (A) brace
   - (B) group
   - (C) chose
   - (D) threw

2. What is most likely the author's purpose in the second paragraph?
   - (A) to introduce the relationship between Coogan and Chaplin
   - (B) to explain Coogan's many talents
   - (C) to convey the challenges of being a child star
   - (D) to demonstrate how successful Coogan was at a young age

3. What is the meaning of the phrase *down on his luck*?
   - (A) receiving good fortune
   - (B) having a hard time
   - (C) doubling down on a bet
   - (D) relying on luck

4. According to the text, who called Coogan "the greatest young actor in the world"?
   - (A) Charlie Chaplin
   - (B) Coogan himself
   - (C) his fans
   - (D) newspaper reporters

5. How did Coogan get Charlie Chaplin's attention?
   - (A) He wrote him a letter.
   - (B) He was a great singer.
   - (C) He was a great impersonator.
   - (D) He auditioned for Chaplin's movie.

6. Which of these statements from the text is an opinion?
   - (A) Coogan was a millionaire before he turned ten.
   - (B) Coogan was great at mimicking other people.
   - (C) He appeared in a few silent movies as well as in vaudeville.
   - (D) Coogan started performing at the age of three.

Name: _____ Date: _____

Directions: Read the text, and answer the questions.

As You Read
Underline all the unfortunate things that happened to Jackie Coogan.

Robbed

Jackie Coogan experienced a few hardships in his life. At the age of 20, his father died in a tragic accident. A year later, he came of age, and he was allowed to use the money he had earned. He was thought to be worth an estimated $50 million (in today's dollars). But when he went to use his money, he found out that most of it was gone. He learned that when his mother remarried, shortly after his father's death, his mother and stepfather had taken his money. They had squandered nearly all of it on expensive cars and fur coats! Coogan sued them. In court, his mother said he didn't deserve the money. Coogan won, but he was only able to retrieve around $100,000 of the millions he had earned. No longer a star, Coogan fell into financial hardship.

This mistreatment led to California passing a law called the Coogan Act. To this day, this law protects child performers from this type of manipulation. It has helped protect child performers from dishonest adults in their lives.

1. Which is closest to the meaning of the phrase *came of age*?
   - (A) became old enough to drive on his own
   - (B) became old enough to know better
   - (C) became old enough to access his savings
   - (D) became too old for the movies

2. Which event happened last?
   - (A) California passed a law called the Coogan Act.
   - (B) Coogan won his court case.
   - (C) Coogan lost his father in an accident.
   - (D) Coogan's mother and stepfather squandered his money.

3. What is an antonym for *squandered*?
   - (A) spent
   - (C) spread
   - (B) saved
   - (D) wasted

4. What does the prefix *mis–* mean in *mistreatment*?
   - (A) good
   - (C) bad
   - (B) not
   - (D) beyond

5. What is the author's purpose in explaining Coogan's lawsuit over his money?
   - (A) to entertain the reader
   - (B) to explain why Coogan is famous
   - (C) to explain why California passed a law
   - (D) to make the reader like Coogan's mother

6. Why did Coogan sue his mother and stepfather?
   - (A) Coogan was unhappy that his mother remarried.
   - (B) They spent most of Coogan's money.
   - (C) Coogan spent all of his money.
   - (D) They did not approve of Coogan's acting career.

Directions: Read the text, and answer the questions.

As You Read
Circle the other jobs and activities that some child stars turn to as they grow up.

All Grown Up

Some child stars continue acting when they become adults. This is what Coogan did. He appeared in movies and television shows until he retired. Today, he is most remembered for his role as Uncle Fester on *The Addams Family* TV show in the 1960s. He played many roles during his career.

Not all child stars continue acting as adults. This may happen for a variety of reasons. They may take a step back from acting to pursue other jobs. Shirley Temple is one example. She retired from acting in 1950 and changed careers entirely. She became a diplomat and worked with the United Nations. Some child actors stop acting because they have trouble booking roles after they grow up. But typically, child actors who quit acting do so because the job has a lot of pressure. At times, it can be a difficult experience. Although many child actors do find a way to stay in the spotlight long after their childhoods, for plenty of others, early retirement is the way to go.

1. What point does the author support with the first paragraph?
   - (A) Coogan was able to retire early like he wanted.
   - (B) Coogan was not forgotten for his childhood roles.
   - (C) Coogan was able to continue working as a successful actor.
   - (D) Coogan became famous at a young age.

2. Is this a dependent or an independent clause? *for plenty of others, early retirement is the way to go.*
   - (A) dependent
   - (B) independent

3. What is one difference between Jackie Coogan and Shirley Temple?
   - (A) Temple acted in movies, Coogan did not.
   - (B) Temple was not a child actor.
   - (C) Temple was forced to stop acting.
   - (D) Temple had multiple careers, while Coogan acted.

4. Which statement would this author likely agree with?
   - (A) Being a child actor can have complicated long-term effects.
   - (B) Being a child actor always leads to a long acting career.
   - (C) Being a child actor is a bad idea.
   - (D) Being a child actor is fun.

5. Summarize the choices that child actors have (or don't have) as they get older.

_____
_____
_____

Name: _____ Date: _____

As You Read

Write thoughts or questions you have about the text in the margins.

A Unique Experience

To some people, acting seems like a very fun profession. Countless child actors have gone on to make majorly successful movies and television shows. But while their lives may seem fun and glamourous, more goes on behind the scenes than you may think.

To start with, child actors do not experience the same type of childhood as non-actors. This is because acting is a very intense and high-pressure job. Although there are laws in place to prevent child actors from working too long, being on set all day is like having a part-time or a full-time job. Imagine having to work between six to eight hours *and* go to middle school. That's often the reality for child actors! When they are filming, they usually have to do schoolwork during breaks on set. They may miss entire weeks or months of school, so they don't get to have a normal school experience. Some child actors are entirely

homeschooled because that can be easier for their filming schedules. In rare cases, some child actors did not even want to act in the first place. It may have been their mom or dad's idea, and they may want to spend their time doing something else. The reality is that acting is a very high-pressure job, and it comes with a lot of expectations. These days, every move an actor makes can be scrutinized online. This can lead to burnout if a child actor is not in the care of responsible adults.

Although acting as a child can have some downsides, there are also many positives. First, child actors usually become close friends with the people on set. This is because all the actors and crew work very closely together, day after day. They can work together for anywhere between a few weeks to a few months. This allows child actors to form very close relationships with their costars. Also, child actors may be able to travel a lot. Sometimes, they need to go to faraway locations for filming. They may be able to experience or do more things than other children their age. Finally, some child stars gain lots of industry experience on set. They may be able to have future job opportunities beyond acting. Some child stars who find fame into adulthood do so by pivoting. For example, when they are older, they may make it in a different career, such as singing, directing, or writing.

Child actors have different experiences than regular children. There are many benefits and downsides to this unique job. Child actor Mary-Kate Olsen once told a reporter, "I would never wish my upbringing on anyone, but I wouldn't take it back for the world."

Directions: Read "A Unique Experience." Then, answer the questions.

1. What is a synonym for *pivoting* as it is used in the text?

   (A) stopping
   (B) spinning
   (C) changing
   (D) renewing

2. What best describes the author's attitude toward parents of child stars?

   (A) skeptical
   (B) proud
   (C) confused
   (D) resentful

3. What does it mean to *make it* as an adult star?

   (A) to build
   (B) to succeed
   (C) to try
   (D) to fail

4. What do the details in paragraph three explain about acting as a child?

   (A) what child actors do as adults
   (B) the types of roles of child actors
   (C) the negatives of child acting
   (D) the positives of child acting

5. What is the meaning of *scrutinized*?

   (A) praised
   (B) examined closely
   (C) misunderstood
   (D) told lies

6. Does the word *high-pressure* have a positive or negative connotation as used in the text?

   (A) positive
   (B) negative

7. Record the positives and negatives of being a child actor discussed in the text.

Positives	Negatives

Name: _____ **Date:** _____

Directions: Reread "A Unique Experience." Then, respond to the prompt.

> Should children be allowed to work as full-time actors? Why or why not? What restrictions do you think should be in place to protect them?

_____
_____
_____
_____
_____
_____
_____
_____
_____
_____
_____
_____
_____
_____
_____
_____
_____
_____
_____
_____
_____
_____
_____
_____

Directions: Read the text, and answer the questions.

Going Viral

It didn't dawn on Nichelle that her life might change forever until she received a phone call from her grandmother all the way in Jamaica.

"Darling, everyone here is watching your video," she said. Nichelle thought to herself, *If my grandma saw Mac's video, I must be going viral*!

The whole thing started off as a joke. Her friend, Mac, was always teasing her about how she sang everywhere she went. Nichelle sang on the bus in the mornings, in the hallway between classes, and sometimes even during class. Her father always asked her politely to refrain from singing at the dinner table, but otherwise, her parents said they liked hearing her sing. Her mother especially loved praising her and said she sang amazingly well.

One comment on social media said that Nichelle must have a four-octave range. Nichelle had never heard the term before, so she looked up what that meant. And it basically meant she was going to be a star!

1. What is an antonym for *viral* as it is used in the text?
   - (A) healthy
   - (B) unknown
   - (C) spreading
   - (D) thriving

2. What is the meaning of the phrase *It didn't dawn on Nichelle*?
   - (A) Nichelle woke up late.
   - (B) Nichelle wasn't told.
   - (C) Nichelle didn't want it to happen.
   - (D) Nichelle didn't consider the possibility.

3. How is this text written?
   - (A) in first person
   - (B) in second person
   - (C) in third person
   - (D) it varies

4. What line from the text provides the best evidence that Nichelle received a positive response to her video?
   - (A) It started off as a joke.
   - (B) It didn't dawn on Nichelle that her life might change forever.
   - (C) It basically meant she was going to be a star.
   - (D) Nichelle sang on the bus in the mornings.

5. Which of these words is not used as an adverb in this text?
   - (A) everyone
   - (B) forever
   - (C) politely
   - (D) amazingly

6. What is the best description of Nichelle's mood in the text?
   - (A) upset
   - (B) annoyed
   - (C) confused
   - (D) surprised

Name: _____ Date: _____

Directions: Read the text, and answer the questions.

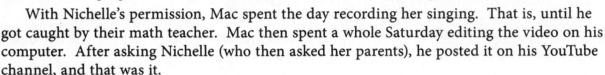

As You Read

Underline descriptions of Nichelle's singing or how people react to it.

The Video

The idea for the video began on the corner where all the kids in Nichelle's neighborhood waited for the bus. Everyone was grumbling about the weather and the fact that the bus was late again. Nichelle started humming a few bars of a song she had made up in her head. Then, she began singing it out loud, mostly to herself. Mac took his phone out to record her, and as he did, the crowd quieted. They all turned their heads to listen to Nichelle, and then they started clapping to the beat of the song! It continued when the bus came, and the other kids picked up the chorus and started singing along. But no amount of amateur singing from a bunch of middle school kids could disguise the real talent.

With Nichelle's permission, Mac spent the day recording her singing. That is, until he got caught by their math teacher. Mac then spent a whole Saturday editing the video on his computer. After asking Nichelle (who then asked her parents), he posted it on his YouTube channel, and that was it.

Well, apparently that it wasn't the end of it. It was just the beginning.

1. What kind of sentence is this? *But no amount of amateur singing from a bunch of middle school kids could disguise the real talent.*
   - Ⓐ simple
   - Ⓑ compound
   - Ⓒ complex
   - Ⓓ compound-complex

2. What is this passage mostly about?
   - Ⓐ where Nichelle learned to sing
   - Ⓑ how the video of Nichelle was created
   - Ⓒ how Nichelle's parents felt about the video
   - Ⓓ why Nichelle decided to make a video

3. Who does *they* refer to in the sixth sentence?
   - Ⓐ Nichelle and Mac
   - Ⓑ Nichelle and her parents
   - Ⓒ all the students at her bus stop
   - Ⓓ all the students on the bus

4. Which of these events happened second?
   - Ⓐ Other students began to sing along.
   - Ⓑ The bus was late.
   - Ⓒ Mac recorded Nichelle and the crowd.
   - Ⓓ Nichelle started singing to herself.

5. What does the author contrast the *amateur singing* of the crowd with?
   - Ⓐ famous singers
   - Ⓑ clapping along to the beat
   - Ⓒ other YouTube stars
   - Ⓓ Nichelle's real talent

6. Which statement is supported by the text?
   - Ⓐ Mac didn't ask before uploading the video.
   - Ⓑ Nobody noticed Nichelle singing.
   - Ⓒ Mac deserves some of the credit for the viral video.
   - Ⓓ The video was uploaded immediately.

Directions: Read the text, and answer the questions.

Social Media Star

Nichelle's and Mac's friends started liking the video, and then a day or two later, Nichelle noticed that the video had over 1,000 views.

Whoa! she thought to herself, *that's a lot.* But she assumed it was just her family and friends watching it over and over again. A few days later, after she received the call from her grandmother, she started feeling a little excited and scared. Nichelle's parents were always busy, so they hadn't really noticed what was going on. When a producer from the late-night show they liked called to ask them if Nichelle could perform for the show, they were aghast! Nichelle had to explain to her parents how the video they agreed to let Mac post had gone viral. Once they understood, her mom squealed and started jumping up and down in excitement, while her dad gasped.

"We're going to Los Angeles," Nichelle's mom chanted. She stopped almost mid-jump, and then said, "Well, we're going to Los Angeles only if you really want to. It's a lot to think about."

Nichelle had a funny feeling in her stomach, but she knew this opportunity was special. "Of course I do!" she told them.

1. What is an antonym for *aghast*?
- (A) horrified
- (B) delighted
- (C) surprised
- (D) annoyed

2. When did Nichelle's parents find out about the video's popularity?
- (A) when it hit over 1,000 views
- (B) when Mac told them
- (C) when Nichelle's grandmother called
- (D) when the producer called

3. Why did Nichelle's mom stop mid-jump?
- (A) She changed her mind about going.
- (B) She realized they needed to ask Nichelle.
- (C) She realized it would be expensive.
- (D) She injured herself.

4. What can you infer about Nichelle's relationships with her parents?
- (A) Her parents respect her.
- (B) Her parents control her.
- (C) Her parents let her boss them around.
- (D) Her parents don't get along with Nichelle.

5. Make a prediction about what will happen in Los Angeles, and explain your reasoning.

_____

_____

_____

Name: _____ Date: _____

To Be...or Not to Be

A few days before her TV appearance, Nichelle sat on her front porch with Mac.

Mac told her, "You're going to be famous—this is exactly what happened to Justin Bieber when he was posting stuff on YouTube. Then, you're going to move to LA, get a recording contract, and years from now, when I have kids, I can tell them that I knew Nichelle before she was famous!"

They laughed about it, but that funny feeling Nichelle had in her stomach got more intense in that moment. It was like a weird knot that wouldn't go away. It was still there when she and her parents boarded their flight to Los Angeles a few days later.

Once they landed and got to the filming studio, Nichelle had to sing one of her favorite songs in front of the most people she had ever sung in front of. Then, she sat down with the host and had to answer all his rapid-fire questions about going viral, if she had a recording contract yet, and when she was moving to LA.

Nichelle's head felt like it was spinning, and when she got back on the plane that night, Nichelle couldn't even remember answering any of the questions. She just knew that the funny feeling in her stomach still hadn't gone away.

The day after Nichelle's performance aired on TV, it felt like the world turned upside-down. When she absentmindedly started singing at the bus stop, someone muttered, "We get it, you're famous." Mac barely stood up for her, which was unusual for him. At lunch, he was sullen and downright grumpy. Nichelle asked him what the problem was, but she had an idea it was about her TV appearance.

He said, "I know I was laughing about you becoming famous, but I'm really going to miss you. You're my best friend, and I almost feel angry that I posted that video."

Nichelle didn't know what to say, but when she started crying, Mac said he was sorry.

That night, Nichelle's dad played a phone message from a record producer who wanted to set up a meeting. Nichelle described how she had been feeling to her parents, and her dad said, "Honey, I'm so sorry; we didn't realize you felt this way. You don't have to do anything you don't want to do, even if that means you never want to sing another note ever again."

Nichelle texted Mac a few minutes later. "Do me a favor, and take down the video."

"Why?" he responded.

"I'm not ready for this. I just want to be normal for now."

"Okay...See you at the bus tomorrow?"

"You bet," Nichelle answered, realizing suddenly that her stomach felt wonderful.

Directions: Read "To Be…or Not to Be." Then, answer the questions.

1. What is a good synonym for *sullen* as used in the text?

   (A) confused
   (B) bright
   (C) cheerful
   (D) gloomy

2. Which word is the best description of how Mac responds before Nichelle appears on TV?

   (A) angry
   (B) supportive
   (C) surprised
   (D) amused

3. How does Mac feel after Nichelle returns home?

   (A) the same as before
   (B) more positive than before
   (C) more upset than before
   (D) he doesn't feel anything

4. What kind of sentence is this? *"You bet," Nichelle answered, realizing suddenly that her stomach felt wonderful.*

   (A) simple
   (B) compound
   (C) complex
   (D) compound-complex

5. What part of speech is the word *downright* in this phrase: *he was sullen and downright grumpy?*

   (A) adjective   (C) noun
   (B) adverb   (D) preposition

6. Why does Nichelle's stomach suddenly feel wonderful?

   (A) She has recovered from illness.
   (B) She is happy that Mac is not mad at her.
   (C) She is excited about her singing career.
   (D) She is relieved to go back to the way things were.

7. Write words and phrases that describe how Nichelle feels and acts before, during, and after her TV appearance.

Before TV	On TV	Afterwards

Name: _____ **Date:** _____

Directions: Reread "To Be...or Not to Be." Then, respond to the prompt.

> Would you like to be famous? Why or why not? If you had to choose one thing to be famous for, what would it be?

_____

_____

_____

_____

_____

_____

_____

_____

_____

_____

_____

_____

_____

_____

_____

_____

_____

_____

_____

_____

_____

_____

_____

_____

_____

_____

This Video Is Unavailable

SUBSCRIBE

 Voiceofreason 10 minutes ago
Everyone listen up! This kid is 12 or 13 years old. Imagine you were her age reading all this garbage about her. Please be kind in your comments!

 Cristina Lynn 1 day ago
Where'd it go? I wanted to show the video to my daughter because she has a great voice. We're going to put a video up soon and get famous just like Nichelle.

 Untidy 8 minutes ago
Don't waste your time. I bet this is a publicity stunt.

 Tierra W 3 days ago
Glad it's gone. I didn't like her video at all.

 SnackAttack 3 days ago
Nichelle really makes the song her own. She's hitting high notes only the most talented of singers can hit, and her phrasing is expressive, creative, and pitch-perfect.

 GGGrayson 3 days ago
I bet some record company signed Nichelle and she had to remove the video. Good luck, Nichelle! I am your biggest fan.

 Untidy 6 days ago
Overrated! I bet they used that autotune.

 Noname Gamer 7 days ago
This kid has potential!

 Untidy 7 days ago
What are you, a talent agent?

 KingKong 7 days ago
I looooove Nichelle and can't wait for her album.

Name: _____   Date: _____

Directions: Read "This Video Is Unavailable." Then, answer the questions.

1. How many different people wrote negative comments or responses?
   - (A) two
   - (B) three
   - (C) six
   - (D) eight

2. Which of the following was not praised by SnackAttack?
   - (A) Nichelle's high notes
   - (B) Nichelle's pitch
   - (C) Nichelle's facial expressions
   - (D) Nichelle's creativity

3. What is the best summary of the responses to Nichelle's video?
   - (A) Most were positive, but some were negative.
   - (B) Most were negative, but some were positive.
   - (C) All were positive.
   - (D) All were negative.

4. What is the tone of Untidy's comments?
   - (A) encouraging
   - (B) accusatory
   - (C) critical
   - (D) helpful

5. Which commenter was particularly concerned with how Nichelle might feel after reading the comments?
   - (A) SnackAttack
   - (B) Voiceofreason
   - (C) KingKong
   - (D) Noname Gamer

6. Which commenter was inspired to upload their own video?
   - (A) Cristina Lynn
   - (B) Untidy
   - (C) KingKong
   - (D) GGGrayson

7. If you were Nichelle, how would you feel after reading these comments? Why?

_____

_____

_____

_____

_____

_____

Directions: Closely read these paragraphs. Then, study the comments on page 23. Look for words describing the positives and negatives of online interactions in each text. Write the words in the chart.

Close-Reading Texts

Social Media Star	To Be...or Not To Be
Nichelle's and Mac's friends started liking the video, and then a day or two later, Nichelle noticed that the video had over 1,000 views. *Whoa!* she thought to herself, *that's a lot.* But she assumed it was just her family and friends watching it over and over again. A few days later, after she received the call from her grandmother, she started feeling a little excited and scared. Nichelle's parents were always busy, so they hadn't really noticed what was going on. When a producer from the late-night show they liked called to ask them if Nichelle could perform for the show, they were aghast! Nichelle had to explain to her parents how the video they agreed to let Mac post had gone viral. Once they understood, her mom squealed and started jumping up and down in excitement, while her dad gasped.	The day after Nichelle's performance aired on TV, it felt like the world turned upside-down. When she absentmindedly started singing at the bus stop, someone muttered, "We get it, you're famous." Mac barely stood up for her, which was unusual for him. At lunch, he was sullen and downright grumpy. Nichelle asked him what the problem was, but she had an idea it was about her TV appearance. He said, "I know I was laughing about you becoming famous, but I'm really going to miss you. You're my best friend, and I almost feel angry that I posted that video." Nichelle didn't know what to say, but when she started crying, Mac said he was sorry.

Text	Positives about Online Interactions	Negatives about Online Interactions
Social Media Star		
To Be...or Not To Be		
This Video Is Unavailable		

Name: _____ Date: _____

Directions: Closely read these passages. Then, compare and contrast the way in which both texts describe what it's like to be famous as a child.

Close-Reading Texts

A Unique Experience	To Be...or Not to Be
To start with, child actors do not experience the same type of childhood as non-actors. This is because acting is a very intense and high-pressure job. Although there are laws in place to prevent child actors from working too long, being on set all day is like having a part-time or a full-time job. Imagine having to work six to eight hours *and* go to middle school. That's often the reality for child actors! When they are filming, they usually have to do schoolwork during breaks on set. They may miss entire weeks or months of school, so they don't get to have a normal school experience. Some child actors are entirely homeschooled because that can be easier for their filming schedules. In rare cases, some child actors did not even want to act in the first place. It may have been their mom or dad's idea, and they may want to spend their time doing something else. The reality is that acting is a very high-pressure job, and it comes with a lot of expectations. These days, every move an actor makes can be scrutinized online. This can lead to burnout if a child actor is not in the care of responsible adults.	Mac told her, "You're going to be famous—this is exactly what happened to Justin Bieber when he was posting stuff on YouTube. Then, you're going to move to LA, get a recording contract, and years from now, when I have kids, I can tell them that I knew Nichelle before she was famous!" They laughed about it, but that funny feeling Nichelle had in her stomach got more intense in that moment. It was like a weird knot that wouldn't go away. It was still there when she and her parents boarded their flight to Los Angeles a few days later. Once they landed and got to the filming studio, Nichelle had to sing one of her favorite songs in front of the most people she had ever sung in front of. Then, she sat down with the host and had to answer all his rapid-fire questions about going viral, if she had a recording contract yet, and when she was moving to LA. Nichelle's head felt like it was spinning, and when she got back on the plane that night, Nichelle couldn't even remember answering any of the questions. She just knew that the funny feeling in her stomach still hadn't gone away.

A Unique Experience   To Be...or Not to Be

Name: _____ **Date:** _____

Directions: Think about the texts from this unit. Then, respond to the prompt.

Should parents allow or encourage children to become stars? Explain your reasoning. Refer to quotations from the texts as evidence to support your argument.

_____

_____

_____

_____

_____

_____

_____

_____

_____

_____

_____

_____

_____

_____

_____

_____

_____

_____

_____

_____

_____

_____

_____

_____

Name: _____ **Date:** _____

Directions: Reread "This Video Is Unavailable." Choose one of the child stars that you read about in Week 1 or 2. Create a fictional page for them on social media. Include posts and comments from fans and critics.

Directions: Read the text, and answer the questions.

As You Read
Circle every god or goddess that is mentioned.

Greek Mythology 2,700 Years Later

Do the names Zeus, Poseidon, or Apollo ring a bell? How about Hercules, Atlas, or Athena? Even if you've never read a Greek myth, you have likely heard of some of these heroes from these ancient stories. Just how ancient are they? The earliest Greek myths go back more than 2,700 years! These stories and legends are ancient. But they are still compelling to many people today. Greek myths cover a variety of topics. Numerous tales tell of Mount Olympus, the tallest mountain of Greece. In Greek myths, it is the home of the ancient god Zeus and his siblings. Greek myths follow these gods on their adventures.

Ideas found in Greek mythology continue to influence our culture, ideas, and entertainment. One need only look at a bestselling books list to see Rick Riordan's Percy Jackson series. These books feature Greek gods, demi-gods, and more. Several movies have been made about Greek mythology, including *Hercules*. It introduced a generation of children to kid-friendly versions of Hercules, Perseus, Achilles, centaurs, and nymphs.

1. Why was Mount Olympus important in Greek mythology?

  Ⓐ It was the capital of ancient Greece.

  Ⓑ It was the home of the ancient Greek gods.

  Ⓒ It was the largest volcano in Greece.

  Ⓓ It was covered in snow.

2. What does the prefix *demi-* mean?

  Ⓐ extra

  Ⓑ against

  Ⓒ half

  Ⓓ all

3. Which word or phrase could best replace *introduced* in the last sentence?

  Ⓐ exposed

  Ⓑ found

  Ⓒ toured

  Ⓓ overlooked

4. Why did the author mention the Percy Jackson series?

  Ⓐ to convey the importance of Zeus in Greek myths

  Ⓑ to demonstrate why ancient Greek authors wrote stories

  Ⓒ to provide an example of a famous Greek god

  Ⓓ to demonstrate the influence of Greek myths on culture today

5. According to the text, how do children today usually get introduced to Greek mythology?

  Ⓐ in school

  Ⓑ through books and movies

  Ⓒ through popular music

  Ⓓ through oral history

6. What can you infer about Zeus?

  Ⓐ He was the youngest.

  Ⓑ He was the most important.

  Ⓒ He had exactly 10 siblings.

  Ⓓ He was a demi-god.

Name: _____ **Date:** _____

Directions: Read the text, and answer the questions.

As You Read

Underline every word used to describe Nike the shoe brand.
Circle every word used to describe Nike the goddess.

The Sneaker God?

Quick! Think of a sneaker brand. Chances are the first company that comes into your head is Nike. It has been one of the most popular and successful sneaker companies for years. Interestingly enough, its name is actually rooted in Greek mythology.

Founded by Phil Knight and Bill Bowerman in 1964, Nike was first called Blue Ribbon Sports. However, no one was satisfied with that. By 1971, when they were ready to market their shoes, they wanted to find a better name. Just five hours before their deadline, one of their employees came up with the name Nike. Nike is the Greek goddess of victory, and according to myth, ancient athletes used to pray to her before they competed. In some depictions, Nike is shown as having wings on her back, which look quite similar to the Nike logo.

Nike has had more influence beyond sneakers, too. Look no further than the 2020 Summer Olympic medals, where Nike is shown as a winged goddess!

1. Why was Nike a good name for a sneaker company?
   - (A) It was the name of the god of speed.
   - (B) It was the site of the first Greek Olympics.
   - (C) It means *fast* in Greek.
   - (D) It was the name of the goddess of victory.

2. Which of the following words is an adverb?
   - (A) ready
   - (B) interestingly
   - (C) popular
   - (D) successful

3. Is this an independent or dependent clause? *Founded by Phil Knight and Bill Bowerman in 1964*
   - (A) dependent
   - (B) independent

4. What is closest to the meaning of *chances are* in this text?
   - (A) It's risky.
   - (B) It's unlikely.
   - (C) It's most likely.
   - (D) It's random.

5. Which of these events occurred first?
   - (A) The Greek Gods were worshipped.
   - (B) The 2020 Olympics took place.
   - (C) Phil Knight and Bill Bowerman founded Blue Ribbon Sports.
   - (D) Nike became the new name of the sneaker company.

6. Which of these statements would the author most likely agree with?
   - (A) Blue Ribbon Sports was a better name for a sneaker company.
   - (B) Nike makes the best sneakers.
   - (C) Nike has always been the most popular sneaker brand.
   - (D) Nike was a sensible choice to name a sneaker company.

Directions: Read the text, and answer the questions.

As You Read
Underline every power or responsibility given to gods or goddesses.

Inspiration from the Ancient Gods

Greek mythology is often a source of inspiration for names. Companies, governments, and many other people take inspiration from characters in Greek myths.

Pandora is one example of this. In Greek mythology, she was the first woman ever created. She was given a box that contained all the world's misery and evil. Pandora was told not to open it, but she was curious, of course. It gnawed away at her for years. Eventually, she opened the box, and all the bad stuff came out. Pandora's name represents someone who was free-spirited and did as she pleased. A jewelry company and an online radio company took inspiration from her name.

Many Greek gods have inspired names as well. For example, Aphrodite is the goddess of beauty, and her symbol is a dove. A beauty care brand's name takes inspiration from her symbol. Ceres is the god of grain, which is where the word *cereal* comes from. Finally, Apollo is a god of many things, including music, art, and archery. When the U.S. space program was looking for a name for their moon project, they chose Apollo. They chose it because as an archer, Apollo never missed his target.

1. What is a good synonym for *free-spirited* as it is used in this text?
   - (A) independent
   - (B) alone
   - (C) impartial
   - (D) unbiased

2. Why did the US space program use the name Apollo?
   - (A) They wanted the program to be fast.
   - (B) They wanted the program to save money.
   - (C) They wanted the program to reach its target, the moon.
   - (D) They wanted the program to inspire the arts.

3. What can you infer from the text?
   - (A) All Greek gods and goddesses are equally inspiring.
   - (B) The names of Greek gods are popular because of their sounds.
   - (C) The meanings of names are important to people.
   - (D) The author prefers names that are not inspired by Greek gods.

4. What is the tone of this passage?
   - (A) humorous
   - (B) sentimental
   - (C) critical
   - (D) informative

5. Write a proposal for a business that might use the name of a Greek god as inspiration. Which Greek god would you choose, and what would be the product?

_____

_____

_____

_____

The Olympics

According to Greek mythology, Nike was the goddess of victory. She awarded athletes with wreaths that she placed on their heads. Thousands of years later, this tradition lives on. At Olympic medal ceremonies, the top athletes bow their heads to receive medals. Many ancient traditions are alive and well at the modern Olympics.

First, the name *Olympics* comes from ancient Greece. The word *Olympus* means "home of the gods." In mythology, it's the name of the mountain peak where Zeus sat on this throne in the clouds. The ancient Greek city of Olympia took its name from this word as well. In the 8th century BCE, a series of competitions were held in Olympia. Athletes from all the city-states of ancient Greece and its colonies traveled to compete. These were considered to be the very first Olympic Games. And today, the name still stands!

There are quite a few similarities between the ancient Olympics and the modern Olympics. For starters, the Olympics today are held every four years, just like the ancient games. Second, the competition has always been open to people from far away. The ancient Greeks welcomed athletes from all their states and colonies. Some people even came to Greece from as far away as modern-day Spain and Turkey! The modern Olympics allow athletes worldwide to compete in the Olympics. Third, as for the actual games, people still compete in some of the same events as the ancient Greeks did. This includes running, discus throwing, and javelin throwing. Finally, prizes play a part at the end of the Olympics. In modern times, the top athletes receive medals after competing. In ancient times, top athletes received various prizes, including olive oil, money, and bronze statuettes. Statues were erected of some of the most famous athletes.

There are also some differences between the modern and ancient Olympics. Summer Olympics and Winter Olympics are held today. Meanwhile, the ancient games only had the singular Olympic event. This difference is due to the huge variety of sports in modern times. For example, skiing and ice skating had not been invented yet in ancient times, so there was no need for a separate winter event. Also, the ancient Olympics could get violent. One ancient sport called *pankration* was similar to today's mixed martial arts. The goal was to kick, wrestle, and box your way to victory any way you could. If you bit your opponent or gouged their eyes, the referee could beat you with a stick. There was no time limit to this event, and sometimes, it was a fight to the death.

The Olympics have a deeply rooted history. Events and ceremonies follow many traditions. One thing remains the same between modern and ancient Olympics: a big win could lead to fame and fortune!

Directions: Read "The Olympics." Then, answer the questions.

1. Which of these statements is a fact supported by the text?
   - (A) Many of the Olympic events today come from the ancient games.
   - (B) Athletes in the modern Olympics become more famous.
   - (C) The ancient Olympics were more exciting.
   - (D) Pankration was less dangerous than mixed martial arts.

2. Which is the best synonym for *gouged* in this text?
   - (A) squeezed
   - (B) poked
   - (C) tore
   - (D) chopped

3. According to the text, what might cause a referee to beat you with a stick in the ancient Olympic games?
   - (A) disrespectful behavior
   - (B) biting someone
   - (C) losing the game
   - (D) taunting your opponent

4. Which of these was not a prize in the ancient Greek Olympics?
   - (A) medals
   - (B) olive oil
   - (C) bronze statuettes
   - (D) money

5. True or false? Ancient Olympian athletes who competed sometimes died.
   - (A) true
   - (B) false

6. Record the similarities and differences between the ancient and modern Olympics.

	Similarities	Differences
Events		
Rules		
Prizes		
Competitors		

Name: _____ **Date:** _____

Directions: Reread "The Olympics." Then, respond to the prompt.

> Imagine you are an Olympic athlete. Would you rather compete in the ancient or modern Olympics? Explain your reasons.

_____

_____

_____

_____

_____

_____

_____

_____

_____

_____

_____

_____

_____

_____

_____

_____

_____

_____

_____

_____

_____

_____

_____

_____

Directions: Read the text, and answer the questions.

As You Read
Underline anything that describes what might happen during the unveiling.

Powers of the Gods

My name is Steph, and today is my unveiling. In my town, anyone who reaches the age of 13 during the year meets at the circle of ancient stones behind the library. This is the ordained day where we receive our individual gifts. My older sister told me that the sacred ceremony wouldn't take long. She says that it reminded her a little bit of superhero movies, when the characters discover what superpowers they have. Lately, I've been feeling that it's more similar to Greek myths in which the sons and daughters of gods end up with special powers.

It's a complete surprise which power you receive at the unveiling. Sometimes, the powers are awesome. I mean, who doesn't like being able to cast lightning bolts up into the air—or into a crowd of bullies. (Don't worry, they don't die; they just become uncomfortable for a little while.) Some kids end up being able to snap their fingers and spin a giant spider web like Anansi. I'm nervous but also excited to see what I will end up with!

1. Which of these is a compound sentence?

   (A) My name is Steph, and today is my unveiling.

   (B) This is the ordained day where we receive our individual gifts.

   (C) Sometimes, the powers are awesome.

   (D) In my town, anyone who reaches the age of 13 during the year meets at the circle of ancient stones behind the library.

2. What genre is this text?

   (A) realistic fiction

   (B) historical fiction

   (C) nonfiction

   (D) fantasy

3. What is the best antonym for the word *ordained*?

   (A) ignored   (C) chosen

   (B) approved   (D) commanded

4. Which is the most likely reason Steph feels nervous?

   (A) The ceremony is dangerous.

   (B) She does not know what to expect.

   (C) She is afraid she won't like her powers.

   (D) She has a specific power she wants.

5. What do you know about Steph based on the text?

   (A) She goes to school with her sister.

   (B) She is 13 this year.

   (C) She has an unusual gift.

   (D) She has a mean older sister.

Name: _____ Date: _____

Directions: Read the text, and answer the questions.

As You Read

Write predictions in the margins. Underline the words and phrases that prompted your predictions.

Origin Story

As for how this all came to be, no one knows for sure. But around seven years ago, while a construction crew was digging up the foundations of an old, abandoned house, they found an ancient rock formation. When the crane operator's 13-year-old son walked over to help investigate, he turned into a cow! Funnily enough, nothing happened to the rest of the adults. After doctors, historians, and scientists in our town did some research, they learned that the rock formation had ancient powers. The boy had gained the powers of Loki, the Norse god of mischief. Since then, our town of Olympus, Virginia, has kept a lid on our secret. Only the newly turned teenagers get to visit the rocks on the sacred day.

You might be wondering what we do with our powers. Well, we actually don't do very much with them! We're not allowed to leave the town for fear of the secret getting out. Some people ask for written permission to leave, which takes a lot of approval, and they have to visit with Jeri. Her powers are from Meng Po, the ancient Chinese goddess of forgetfulness. She's a great asset to our town.

1. Why can't the inhabitants of Olympus use their powers freely in the world?
   - Ⓐ They are not strong enough.
   - Ⓑ No one knows for sure.
   - Ⓒ They want to keep it a secret.
   - Ⓓ The powers only work in the town of Olympus.

2. What kind of sentence is this? *As for how this all came to be, no one knows for sure.*
   - Ⓐ simple
   - Ⓑ compound
   - Ⓒ complex
   - Ⓓ compound-complex

3. Which is a synonym for *asset* as it is used in the last sentence?
   - Ⓐ possession
   - Ⓒ qualification
   - Ⓑ boon
   - Ⓓ drawback

4. Which word has a similar meaning to *mischief* but with a more positive connotation?
   - Ⓐ problems
   - Ⓒ hoax
   - Ⓑ help
   - Ⓓ joking

5. What part of speech is *forgetfulness*?
   - Ⓐ verb
   - Ⓑ adjective
   - Ⓒ adverb
   - Ⓓ noun

6. What can you infer about how the inhabitants view outsiders?
   - Ⓐ Outsiders are welcome.
   - Ⓑ Outsiders are threats.
   - Ⓒ Outsiders are not a concern.
   - Ⓓ Outsiders are the cause of all problems.

Name: ______________________________ Date: ____________________

Directions: Read the text, and answer the questions.

As You Read

Circle any words or phrases that give you clues about how Steph is feeling.

The Moment of Truth

Some people say that when you visit the rocks, you'll get the power you secretly ask for. This is why so many teenagers in our town have winged feet and can fly. But when I think about what power to ask for, I feel stumped. I know I want something more helpful than lightning bolts and flying, but I'm just not sure what that could be.

At the unveiling, I exchange excited chatter with my classmates, but I can't help wondering if we could be a part of something greater. The world could really use our special powers, but we're not allowed to leave. In our town, we always have enough rain for our crops thanks to my classmate, Bea. She assumed the powers of Pachamama, the Inka goddess of planting and harvesting crops. But I know there are deserts and drier climates that could really benefit from this power.

I think about this as I watch everyone walk to the center of the rocks and wait. Martha, who got her powers from Thoth, the Egyptian god of time, knows when your time is up. After she says you're done, you stand by the back entrance to the library and wait for your powers to kick in.

1. Which is a synonym for *chatter*?

- (A) yell
- (B) converse
- (C) ask
- (D) challenge

2. Why doesn't Steph want the power to fly?

- (A) She doesn't like the god of flight.
- (B) She is afraid to fly.
- (C) She wants the power of invisibility.
- (D) She wants to be more helpful.

3. Which of these transition words indicates contrast?

- (A) if
- (B) but
- (C) sure
- (D) afterwards

4. What is another good title for this passage?

- (A) Getting to Fly
- (B) Olympus, Virginia
- (C) Testing Our Powers
- (D) The Time Has Come

5. Summarize the events of the story so far.

____

____

____

6. Would you want the power to fly if you lived in this town? Why or why not?

____

____

____

As You Read

Underline words and phrases that tell you about Steph's attitude or emotions.

Superpowers for the World

After some time spent waiting, most of my classmates are zipping around with their winged boots and knocking apples off a nearby tree with their lightning bolts. Nothing, however, has happened to me yet, except for having two dogs run up to me and not leave my side.

Ramesh, who sits next to me in social studies, walks up to me. He tells me that he has received the wisdom of the Indian god Ganesha. He looks at me for a moment and then says, "I can see that you have the powers of Babalu Aye, a god among the Yoruba people of Nigeria and Benin."

Before I can ask him what that means, he says, "Your dogs can sniff out infections and epidemics, and you can cure them."

A few days later, I realize how useful my powers are for our town. I've been hearing a lot about a virus that's going around our town and making people sick. One afternoon, I set up shop at the gazebo in the town center, and everyone walks up to me. The dogs sniff them, I cure them, and soon, no one is sick anymore!

That night, the same ideas I had before swirl around my head: *What about the rest of the world? I can get rid of people's illnesses in no time at all…if only I can get out of this town!*

I ask my parents if I can have permission to leave, but they tell me not to rock the boat or get into trouble. Then, I ask the town council, who forbids me to leave. They threaten to have Jeri wipe my memory if I keep talking about my idea. I'm disappointed by this, but I know that my power would be useful outside my town, so I keep thinking of ways to escape.

One afternoon, while walking my dogs, I come across Alicia, an old friend from elementary school. She's been strangely quiet about her power, and as we walk together for a bit, I ask her if she's okay.

"Well, not really, because my power is strange," she says. "In Roman mythology, Janus is the god of doorways, beginnings, and ends, and I'm not sure what to do about it."

I think about this for a minute, and suddenly I'm struck with an awesome plan. "Alicia, can you make a doorway that lets us leave town without the council finding out?"

"Yeah, that should be really easy, actually. Jeri won't be able to get to us fast enough," she says.

"Do you want to help me save the world?" I ask her.

Alicia stops walking and looks at me with curiosity, her smile widening. "Let me get my coat."

Name: _____ **Date:** _____

Directions: Read "Superpowers for the World." Then, answer the questions.

1. Which is closest to the meaning of *rock the boat*?
   - (A) disturb the status quo
   - (B) get in trouble with the law
   - (C) add the last straw
   - (D) blame someone else

2. What does the prefix *epi–* mean in *epidemic* if the root, *demos*, means people or district?
   - (A) from
   - (B) upon
   - (C) without
   - (D) not

3. Which word best describes Steph's attitude toward her gift?
   - (A) annoyed
   - (B) cavalier
   - (C) indulgent
   - (D) altruistic

4. Why is Steph haunted by questions?
   - (A) She is confused.
   - (B) She wants to help others.
   - (C) She wants different powers.
   - (D) She is not sure what her powers do.

5. What literary device can be found in the title of this passage?
   - (A) hyperbole
   - (B) foreshadowing
   - (C) simile
   - (D) metaphor

6. Which of these statements is true?
   - (A) Steph is content.
   - (B) Alicia is worried about getting caught.
   - (C) Steph wishes she had different powers.
   - (D) Alicia wants to help Steph.

7. Describe the setting, characters, and conflict or problem in the story.

Setting	Characters	Conflict/Problem

Name: _____ **Date:** _____

Directions: Reread "Superpowers for the World." Then, respond to the prompt.

Complete the story two ways. First, create a happy ending. Then, create an unhappy ending.

_____
_____
_____
_____
_____
_____
_____
_____
_____
_____
_____
_____
_____
_____
_____
_____
_____
_____
_____
_____
_____
_____

Olympus TRAVEL BROCHURE

Book Now

Welcome to Mount Olympus, the home of the ancient Greek gods.

According to ancient tradition, only gods are allowed on Olympus, but don't worry. At Imaginary Lands Travel Agency, we have the perfect solution. For the duration of your stay on Olympus, you will be an honorary god or goddess! We hope you enjoy your stay.

This special offer includes:

- your very own godlike name that you can take home with you
- three superpowers of your own choosing
- your very own symbol of power
- temporary immortality
- your own palace, where you will be waited on hand and foot
- special keepsake statue of yourself as a god or goddess
- togas and sandals, of course!

While on Olympus, there are a few guidelines you should follow (if you know what's good for you):

- Don't make fun of Zeus. He doesn't have a sense of humor.
- Remember, you're up high above the clouds, so don't drop anything.
- If you don't like ambrosia and nectar, bring your own snacks.
- If you play checkers with Ares, the god of war, let him win.

Imaginary Lands
TRAVEL AGENCY

Name: _____ Date: _____

Directions: Read "Olympus Travel Brochure." Then, answer the questions.

1. What does the prefix *im–* mean in *immortality*?

(A) extra

(B) not

(C) with

(D) from

2. What is the author implying by *if you know what's good for you*?

(A) You should study before going there.

(B) This trip will be good for you.

(C) The gods will look out for you.

(D) Something bad could happen to you if you disobey.

3. What is the tone of this text?

(A) persuasive

(B) critical

(C) informative

(D) cynical

4. Which is the best ending to this statement, based on the text? *A trip to Olympus would be _____.*

(A) cheap

(B) extraordinary

(C) pedestrian

(D) run-of-the-mill

5. Which of the following is **not** true about one's honorary status as a god or goddess?

(A) You can choose your powers.

(B) It is temporary.

(C) You are immortal.

(D) You can't take anything with you.

6. Which of the following words does **not** relate to time?

(A) temporary

(B) duration

(C) during

(D) according

7. What would you choose as your three superpowers? Why?

_____

_____

_____

_____

_____

_____

_____

_____

_____

_____

_____

Directions: Closely read these paragraphs, and then review the travel brochure on page 41. Examine how they describe the ancient gods and their powers. Record the information in the chart.

Close-Reading Texts

Inspiration from the Ancient Gods	Powers of the Gods
Pandora is one example of this. In Greek mythology, she was the first woman ever created. She was given a box that contained all the world's misery and evil. Pandora was told not to open it, but she was curious, of course. It gnawed away at her for years. Eventually, she opened the box, and all the bad stuff came out. Pandora's name represents someone who was free-spirited and did as she pleased. A jewelry company and an online radio company took inspiration from her name. Many Greek gods have inspired names as well. For example, Aphrodite is the goddess of beauty, and her symbol is a dove. A beauty care brand's name takes inspiration from her symbol. Ceres is the god of grain, which is where the word cereal comes from. Finally, Apollo is a god of many things, including music, art, and archery. When the U.S. space program was looking for a name for their moon project, they chose Apollo. They chose it because as an archer, Apollo never missed his target.	It's a complete surprise which power you receive at the unveiling. Sometimes, the powers are awesome. I mean, who doesn't like being able to cast lightning bolts up into the air-or into a crowd of bullies. (Don't worry, they don't die; they just become uncomfortable for a little while.) Some kids end up being able to snap their fingers and spin a giant spider web like Anansi. I'm nervous but also excited to see what I will end up with!

Text	Descriptions
Inspiration from the Ancient Gods	
Powers of the Gods	
Olympus Travel Brochure	

Name: _____ Date: _____

Directions: Closely read these paragraphs. Contrast the way each text describes godlike powers. For each element, include a description and evidence from the text.

Close-Reading Texts

The Moment of Truth	Olympus Travel Brochure
Some people say that you when you visit the rocks, you'll get the power you secretly ask for. This is why so many teenagers in our town have winged feet and can fly. But when I think about what power to ask for, I feel stumped. I know I want something more helpful than lightning bolts and flying, but I'm just not sure what that could be. At the unveiling, I exchange excited chatter with my classmates, but I can't help wondering if we could be a part of something greater. The world could really use our special powers, but we're not allowed to leave. In our town, we always have enough rain for our crops thanks to my classmate, Bea. She assumed the powers of Pachamama, the Inka goddess of planting and harvesting crops. But I know there are deserts and drier climates that could really benefit from this power.	For the duration of your stay on Olympus, you will be an honorary god or goddess! We hope you enjoy your stay. This special offer includes: • your very own godlike name that you can take home with you • three superpowers of your own choosing • your very own symbol of power • temporary immortality • your own palace, where you will be waited on hand and foot • special keepsake statue of yourself as a god or goddess • togas and sandals, of course!

	The Moment of Truth	Olympus Travel Brochure
Examples of Powers and Other Perks		
Tone of the Passage		
Long-Term Outcome of Receiving Powers		

Name: _____ **Date:** _____

Directions: Think about the texts from this unit. Then, respond to the prompt.

You are on the council for the town of Olympus, Virginia. The council is holding a discussion about whether to allow people to come and go without restrictions. Write a speech outlining your position. Explain your reasons, and be persuasive!

_____

_____

_____

_____

_____

_____

_____

_____

_____

_____

_____

_____

_____

_____

_____

_____

_____

_____

_____

_____

_____

_____

_____

Name: _____ **Date:** _____

Directions: Imagine you have just returned from a trip to Mount Olympus with the Imaginary Lands Travel Agency. Write a review for their website, detailing what happened, what you liked, and what you disliked.

User Name

_____

_____

_____

_____

_____

_____

_____

_____

_____

_____

_____

_____

_____

_____

_____

_____

_____

_____

_____

Was this review . . . ?

| Useful | Funny | Interesting |

Directions: Read the text, and answer the questions.

As You Read
Underline physical descriptions of elephants.

Big Means Big

Elephants are highly intelligent, compassionate, and social animals. But the thing that might grab your attention the most is their appearance. Elephants are massive. They happen to be the largest land mammals on Earth. Male elephants can grow to be 11 feet (3.4 meters) tall at their shoulders. They can weigh up to 7 tons (6,350 kilograms). Next, each elephant has large ears, tusks, and a long trunk. Elephants can do many different things with their trunks. An elephant can lift up to 700 pounds (318 kilograms) with its trunk, but it can also be sensitive enough to pick up a single grape on the ground. An elephant can use its trunk to breathe, smell, reach, trumpet noises of warning or greeting, suck up water, and more! Finally, elephants can run very fast. They can run up to 25 miles (40,233 meters) per hour. Elephants are a sight to behold, and an encounter with one or more can be a memorable experience.

1. Which of these statements from the text is an opinion?
   - Ⓐ They can run up to 25 miles (40,233 meters) per hour.
   - Ⓑ An elephant can lift up to 700 pounds (318 kilograms) with its trunk, but it can also be sensitive enough to pick up a single grape on the ground.
   - Ⓒ Elephants are a sight to behold, and an encounter with one or more can be a memorable experience.
   - Ⓓ An elephant can use its trunk to breathe, smell, reach, trumpet noises of warning or greeting, suck up water, and more!

2. In the first sentence, the adjectives *intelligent*, *compassionate*, and *social* are modifying which word?
   - Ⓐ animals
   - Ⓑ elephants
   - Ⓒ highly
   - Ⓓ attention

3. Which word is the best synonym for the word *trumpet* as it is used in the text?
   - Ⓐ instrument
   - Ⓒ hear
   - Ⓑ horn
   - Ⓓ broadcast

4. Which word best describes the author's attitude toward elephants?
   - Ⓐ veneration
   - Ⓒ ignorance
   - Ⓑ detestation
   - Ⓓ confusion

5. What kind of sentence is this? *Elephants are massive.*
   - Ⓐ simple
   - Ⓒ complex
   - Ⓑ compound
   - Ⓓ compound-complex

6. Which of these statements is **not** true about elephants?
   - Ⓐ They are the largest land mammals.
   - Ⓑ The largest elephants weigh about 5 tons.
   - Ⓒ They can lift hundreds of pounds with their trunks.
   - Ⓓ They can run up to 25 miles per hour.

Name: _____   **Date:** _____

Directions: Read the text, and answer the questions.

Elephant Basics

Elephants have complex social structures that include families of females and calves. Males tend to live alone or in small "bachelor" groups. These family groups can consist of 10 or more members and include calves and their mothers. The eldest female is the leader of the family and acts as the matriarch. Together, they search for food and water and protect the calves by forming a circle around them when relaxing or eating. Elephants mourn the deaths of family members. Just like humans, they experience a grieving process. They also show compassion, and their intelligence is about the same as primates'.

There are three living species of elephants: the African bush elephant, the African forest elephant, and the Asian elephant. Each species is unique. For example, African elephants are larger, have bigger ears, and both the males and females grow tusks. Meanwhile, only some Asian elephant males grow tusks. Humans throughout time have been fascinated by elephants, and they have learned a lot about them through careful study. Why, then, are there so few elephants left in the wild?

1. How many species of elephants are there?
   - (A) one
   - (B) two
   - (C) three
   - (D) four

2. Which word best matches the meaning of the phrase *complex social structures*?
   - (A) families
   - (B) organizations
   - (C) schools
   - (D) buildings

3. Which of the following statements is **not** true?
   - (A) Elephants grieve the deaths of their family members.
   - (B) Elephants are as smart as primates.
   - (C) Asian elephants are larger than African elephants.
   - (D) Male elephants often live alone.

4. What does the root *matr* mean, as in *matriarch*?
   - (A) great
   - (B) order
   - (C) mother
   - (D) leader

5. What can you infer from this sentence? *There are three living species of elephants.*
   - (A) There used to be fewer species.
   - (B) There used to be at least one other species.
   - (C) There are major differences between each species.
   - (D) There are few differences between each species.

6. What would a reader most likely predict the next part of the text will discuss?
   - (A) the diet of an elephant
   - (B) elephant behavior
   - (C) threats to elephants
   - (D) stories about elephants

Directions: Read the text, and answer the questions.

As You Read
Underline all the threats to elephants.

Declining Elephant Populations

In the 1970s, there were more than one million wild elephants in the world. Today, that number is around 400,000 and declining in some areas. There are a couple of key factors in this drop in numbers.

The first reason is the illegal ivory trade. Elephant tusks are like teeth, and they are made of ivory, which is a hard, white material. Ivory has been used for centuries to make jewelry, art, piano keys, and more. Today, it is still highly sought after. But the only way to get ivory is to kill animals who have tusks. Countries around the world have banned the import and export of elephant ivory. This has helped elephant populations rebound. However, illegal hunters called *poachers* still hunt elephants for their ivory.

Another factor that affects elephant populations is their movement. Elephants are known as migratory animals. This means they are always in search of food and water. Elephants need a massive amount of land to roam freely. But more and more often, elephants are met by farms where humans grow crops that elephants love to eat. Elephants accidentally destroy the farms, trying to get enough to eat. This leads to conflict, and all too often, death. Elephant populations are decreasing for these two key reasons.

1. Which word is closest to the meaning of *rebound* in the second paragraph?
- (A) bounce
- (B) recover
- (C) reverberate
- (D) decline

2. How does elephant migration cause conflict?
- (A) Elephants encounter predator animals.
- (B) There is no more vegetation for elephants.
- (C) Elephants fight each other for water.
- (D) Elephants encroach on farmland.

3. What can you infer from this passage?
- (A) Elephants are doing fine.
- (B) Humans are responsible for the decline in elephant populations.
- (C) Elephants are affected by climate change.
- (D) There is general agreement on how to increase elephant populations.

4. The italicized clause in the following sentence from the text is an example of a/an _____ clause. "This leads to conflict, *and all too often*, death."
- (A) dependent
- (B) independent

5. What is the main idea of this passage?

_____
_____
_____

Elephants and Bees: One Solution

As a child growing up in the 1980s, Lucy King spent most of her childhood outdoors. King was from the United Kingdom, but her parents taught in South Africa and Kenya. King and her family went on camping trips where elephants would walk right outside their tent! She learned about decreasing elephant populations, and she knew she wanted to help these giant, beautiful creatures. When King went to college, she studied zoology so she could do everything possible to save elephants and their habitat. She has spent most of her life pursuing this cause.

The main problem King wanted to solve in the South African game parks was the huge electric fences. Elephants were contained within these fences. The fences kept other animals from getting in, and they kept humans and their farms safe from wandering elephants. However, the fences also kept elephants from roaming more freely. And some very smart elephants learned that their trunks didn't conduct electricity, which allowed them to use them to break the fences!

King thought there had to be a better way for elephants and humans to coexist. While studying for her Ph.D., King learned that elephants were really afraid of bees. Even though elephants have very thick skin, wild African bees attacked around elephants' eyes, ears, and mouths, causing painful stings. This aversion to bees gave King an idea she wanted to test out.

beehive fence in Kenya

First, King recorded the sound made by a hive of disturbed, angry bees. Then, she set up a sound system near a family of elephants resting in the shade of a tree. When King played the recording, the elephants' ears went up. Then, they started moving their heads from side to side. One elephant kicked a calf to get it up. Soon, they ran off! King repeated this experiment many times and found that 80 percent of the time, elephants avoided the bee noise.

King's next step was to find farmers willing to build simple fences around their crops with beehives posted every 20 yards (18 meters). Her idea was that elephants would approach the farm and walk into the simple fence's wire. Then, the jiggling wire would wake up the bees, sending the elephants running. King tested her idea, and it worked! Today, dozens of farms are protected by these peacekeeping bees. These farms are in 19 countries, and the farmers are able to protect their crops and make money by selling the honey from the hives.

King's dedication to finding a replacement for the electric fences helped elephants greatly. This natural solution allowed humans and elephants to coexist peacefully. As more wild land is turned into farms, ideas and innovations like King's will be needed to help protect elephants.

Name: _____ Date: _____

Directions: Read "Elephants and Bees: One Solution." Then, answer the questions.

1. What is the meaning of the suffix *-ology* as it is used in the word *zoology*?

   Ⓐ animals

   Ⓑ university

   Ⓒ study of

   Ⓓ environment

2. What did King likely think of the electric fences around South African game parks?

   Ⓐ They were cruel but necessary.

   Ⓑ They were cruel and ineffective.

   Ⓒ They were the best option.

   Ⓓ They were gentle and protective.

3. Why did King record the bees?

   Ⓐ to create better sites for beehives

   Ⓑ to test elephants' reactions to the sound

   Ⓒ to use the sound to attract more bees

   Ⓓ to test how bees responded to elephants

4. Which of these events happened second?

   Ⓐ King noticed that elephants feared bees.

   Ⓑ King noticed that elephants sometimes broke through electric fences.

   Ⓒ King grew up in South Africa and Kenya, around elephants.

   Ⓓ King convinced dozens of farmers to set up bee fences.

5. What kind of sentence is this? *As a kid growing up in the 1980s, Lucy King spent most of her time outdoors.*

   Ⓐ simple

   Ⓑ compound

   Ⓒ complex

   Ⓓ compound-complex

6. Complete this graphic organizer, identifying the pros and cons of two ways to keep elephants out of farmland.

Solution	Pros	Cons
Electric Fences		
Bee Fences		

Name: _____ **Date:** _____

Directions: Reread "Elephants and Bees: One Solution." Then, respond to the prompt.

Consider the pros and cons of each solution. Write a speech that King might give to a farmer to convince them to set up a bee fence.

_____
_____
_____
_____
_____
_____
_____
_____
_____
_____
_____
_____
_____
_____
_____
_____
_____
_____
_____
_____
_____
_____
_____
_____
_____
_____

Name: _____ **Date:** _____

Directions: Read the text, and answer the questions.

As You Read

Underline any behavior that you find strange or surprising.

Playing the Piano with Your Nose

When Arash got home from school one day, instead of heading to the kitchen for a snack, he dropped his backpack in the hallway and ran to his grandmother's old piano. It was a beautiful baby grand that had been in the family for years and years.

"I bought it with my own money from my first job," Arash's grandmother proudly said whenever she sat down to play it. Arash's father was very proud of the piano, too, and he would sometimes sit and play the songs he knew after everyone had eaten dinner.

Arash opened the keyboard cover and stared at the keys. He got so close to them that when his sister Laleh walked through the door, she thought he was trying to play a song with his nose.

"What in the world are you doing, Arash? That's not the best way to play a piano, although I could take a video of you and post it if you want. Maybe you'll go viral!"

"No thanks," Arash replied, "I am just making sure the keys are not made of ivory because I don't want us to break the law."

1. Which word is used as an adverb in the text?

   (A) baby
   (B) best
   (C) through
   (D) very

2. Why is Arash's grandmother proud of the piano?

   (A) It is rare.
   (B) It is her grandson's favorite thing.
   (C) She bought it on her own.
   (D) She taught her son to play it.

3. Based on this passage, what can you infer about Arash?

   (A) He is an excellent piano player.
   (B) He is close to his grandfather.
   (C) He and his sister don't get along.
   (D) He is interested in the piano.

4. Which of these events does **not** happen in this passage?

   (A) Arash drops his backpack.
   (B) Arash has a snack.
   (C) Laleh teases her brother.
   (D) Arash opens the keyboard cover.

5. What kind of sentence is this? *When Arash got home from school one day, instead of heading to the kitchen for a snack, he dropped his backpack in the hallway and ran to his grandmother's old piano.*

   (A) simple
   (B) compound
   (C) complex
   (D) compound-complex

6. What is the author trying to indicate with the word *ran* in the first sentence?

   (A) urgency   (C) hesitation
   (B) vacillation   (D) humor

Name: _____   Date: _____

Directions: Read the text, and answer the questions.

As You Read
Circle all the adverbs, and underline all the adjectives.

No Melty Cheese and Crackers for Arash

Laleh had no idea what Arash was talking about.

"What's so illegal about ivory?" she asked him.

Arash said, "It's illegal to have things made out of ivory! Since this piano is so old, the keys might be made out of ivory, and we could all be going to jail!"

Laleh opened her mouth to respond, but then she saw a book on elephants peeking out of Arash's backpack. *Of course*, she thought to herself, *they probably talked about elephants in science class today*. Laleh asked Arash about it, and he told her that they learned about elephant tusks and the illegal ivory trade.

"Don't worry, nobody is going to come after us for our piano, I promise you," Laleh said. "Now come in the kitchen, and I'll make us melty cheese on crackers."

Melty cheese and crackers was Arash's favorite, but he wasn't going to let his worry go so easily. Instead of following Laleh into the kitchen, he asked her if she had seen his magnifying glass.

1. What is Arash's attitude toward their piano?

- (A) respect
- (B) tedium
- (C) trepidation
- (D) indifference

2. What is Laleh trying to do using the melty cheese and crackers?

- (A) distract Arash
- (B) answer Arash's questions
- (C) reward Arash
- (D) feed herself

3. What outcome is Arash most afraid of?

- (A) losing their piano
- (B) angering his grandmother
- (C) getting arrested
- (D) hurting the elephants

4. Which line from the passage is the best evidence to support the idea that Laleh is trying to calm her brother down?

- (A) "What's so illegal about ivory?" she asked him.
- (B) *Of course*, she thought to herself, *they probably talked about elephants in science class today*
- (C) "Don't worry, nobody is going to come after us for our piano, I promise you," Laleh said.
- (D) Laleh had no idea what Arash was talking about.

5. What can you infer about Arash based on this passage?

- (A) He pays attention in science class.
- (B) He does not care about elephants.
- (C) He thinks his sister is smarter than him.
- (D) He is usually carefree.

Directions: Read the text, and answer the questions.

As You Read

Underline any words that indicate how Arash is feeling.

What a Mess!

Arash ran up to his room, and Laleh could hear him tossing a variety of books and toys around. With a sigh, she trudged up the stairs, knocked on Arash's door, and went inside.

His room was always a disaster even on a good day, so today's mess had made the problem even worse. All the contents of Arash's drawers and bookshelves were scattered on the floor.

"Arash," she said, "Nobody is going to come get us because of our piano keys."

Arash spoke rapidly without stopping to breathe: "But Ms. Soltys said that thousands of elephants are killed every year for their tusks, even though it's illegal! Plus, countries around the world have banned the selling of ivory!"

"Well, there you have it; we're not selling the piano, so there's no problem," Laleh said, hoping to put an end to his worries before their parents got home. As she glanced around the room, she noticed Arash's magnifying glass on the carpet next to her.

"Is this what you're looking for?" she asked, handing it to him.

1. What is a good antonym for the word *banned* as it is used in the passage?

   Ⓐ forbade
   Ⓑ authorized
   Ⓒ controlled
   Ⓓ ignored

2. What kind of connotation does the word *trudged* have?

   Ⓐ positive
   Ⓑ negative
   Ⓒ neutral

3. Which of the following is a compound sentence?

   Ⓐ With a sigh, she trudged up the stairs, knocked on Arash's door, and went inside.
   Ⓑ As she glanced around the room, she noticed Arash's magnifying glass on the carpet next to her.
   Ⓒ All the contents of Arash's drawers and bookshelves were scattered on the floor.
   Ⓓ Arash ran up to his room, and Laleh could hear him tossing a variety of books and toys around.

4. How might Arash alleviate his concerns? What kind of evidence might he need to feel comfortable?

   _____
   _____
   _____
   _____

As You Read
Underline information Arash discovers about the piano's keys.

Ivory in the House

Laleh finally coaxed Arash back down to the kitchen for a snack. She felt bad for how Arash was feeling, and she decided to get out their tablet to do some research. First, she looked up how to tell whether piano keys were made out of ivory. After scanning a few websites, she said, "Arash, if the piano keys are yellow, that could mean they are made of ivory. But this also says that it is not illegal to own an antique that is made of ivory."

Laleh made Arash finish his snack before he could examine the piano with his magnifying glass. Laleh, with the tablet in hand, read out loud, "Ivory has a fine grain you can see if you look closely enough. It's sort of like a fingerprint."

Arash squinted and said, "It's a little yellow, but I can't see any fingerprints."

Laleh said, "Also, it says here that we can heat a sharp needle and poke one of the keys with it. If it goes through the key, it's not ivory."

Arash looked over each key and then confidently told her that the keys were clearly not made of ivory. At that moment, their dad walked through the front door, overhearing their conversation. He laughed and clapped Arash on the back.

"Son, our piano was made after 1950, which was around the time piano makers stopped using ivory," he said. "Even back then, people knew what the ivory trade was doing to the elephant populations. However, even though our piano keys are not made of ivory, I want to show you something that is made of ivory."

They followed their dad over to the china cabinet. He opened one of the doors and took out a small statue of a boy. Their dad explained that the statue belonged to his great-grandfather, and it had been carved out of ivory many, many years ago.

"Oh, no," Arash cried, "We're done for; we're breaking the law for sure!"

Laleh responded, "No, like I told you earlier, it's okay to have antiques like this in the house. But if we feel bad about it, we can donate anything made out of ivory to the U.S. Fish & Wildlife Service. They'll use it to educate the public about the ivory trade and animal conservation."

Their dad said, "You know, I have felt badly about having this statue, so let's give it to them so others can learn."

Arash sighed with relief and said, "Maybe we should send the piano to them too, just to be safe."

"Nice try, Arash, but you'll have to think of some other way to get out of your piano lessons," their dad said.

Directions: Read "Ivory in the House." Then, answer the questions.

1. What is a good synonym for *coaxed* as it is used in the text?

- (A) forced
- (B) told
- (C) coerced
- (D) persuaded

2. Which of the following is **not** an indication that something is made of ivory?

- (A) It is yellow in color.
- (B) It is too hard to poke with a needle.
- (C) It has a visible grain.
- (D) It sinks in water.

3. What does the word *it* refer to in this sentence? *They'll use it to educate the public about the ivory trade and animal conservation.*

- (A) tusks
- (B) information
- (C) the statue
- (D) pianos

4. Why does Arash ask to donate the piano at the end?

- (A) He wants to help educate people.
- (B) He still thinks it is made of ivory.
- (C) He doesn't want to practice piano.
- (D) His father wants him to.

5. Which of these events happens last?

- (A) Arash's father shows them the statue.
- (B) Laleh looks up ways to identify ivory.
- (C) Arash decides the keys are not made of ivory.
- (D) Arash goes to the kitchen for a snack.

6. Record the actions Arash, Laleh, and their father take to resolve the problem.

Problem	Arash is worried about breaking the law.
Steps to a Resolution	

Name: _____ **Date:** _____

Directions: Reread "Ivory in the House." Then, respond to the prompt.

Imagine you are Arash, and your family has returned from a visit to the the U.S. Fish and Wildlife Service. Write a journal entry explaining what happened that day. Consider how you feel and what you see and learn during the visit.

_____
_____
_____
_____
_____
_____
_____
_____
_____
_____
_____
_____
_____
_____
_____
_____
_____
_____
_____
_____
_____

Name: _____ Date: _____

 # ELEPHANT PAINTING NOW

The next time you see a cute elephant painting a picture with its trunk, take a look at who's close by and what they are holding. If a trainer has a tool with a point or a hook on the end, the elephant is being trained to paint using methods that hurt the animal. This device is called a bullhook, and it is used in some American zoos and preserves to train elephants to do tricks. This barbaric device has been prohibited in some cities, but many more still use it.

There are many reasons why these should be banned. First, elephants are not meant to do our bidding! Elephants are wild animals, and they do not paint for fun. They are not expressing their creativity by painting because are not naturally creative. In fact, they are trained to draw, and they need to be coaxed by trainers to produce (usually) the same painting every time!

True sanctuaries for elephants don't force them to do tricks. Ban bullhooks now! Stop elephants from performing tricks! Sign the petition on the next page to help us save the elephants!

Name: _____ **Date:** _____

Directions: Read "Stop Elephant Painting Now." Then, answer the questions.

1. What is the author's purpose in creating this?
   - Ⓐ to entertain
   - Ⓒ to persuade
   - Ⓑ to question
   - Ⓓ to frighten

2. What is a good synonym for the word *barbaric* as it is used in this text?
   - Ⓐ wild
   - Ⓒ brutal
   - Ⓑ gentle
   - Ⓓ spiky

3. Based on this text, which statement would the author likely agree with?
   - Ⓐ Animals should not be forced to entertain people.
   - Ⓑ Animals are not equal to people.
   - Ⓒ Animals are lucky to be cared for by people.
   - Ⓓ Animal artwork should be cherished.

4. Which word has a similar meaning to *coax* but a more negative connotation?
   - Ⓐ persuade
   - Ⓑ convince
   - Ⓒ coerce
   - Ⓓ flatter

5. Which is the best synonym for *sanctuaries* as it is used in this text?
   - Ⓐ hospitals
   - Ⓑ havens
   - Ⓒ hideouts
   - Ⓓ hostel

6. Answer the following questions in the chart. What is the problem according to this text? What solution does the author advocate? What action can the reader take?

Problem	Solution	Action

Name: _____ **Date:** _____

Directions: Closely read these paragraphs. Then, study the poster on page 59. In the chart, record the threats to elephants and the changes needed.

Close-Reading Texts

Declining Elephant Populations	What a Mess!
Another factor that affects elephant populations is their movement. Elephants are known as migratory animals. This means they are always in search of food and water. Elephants need a massive amount of land to roam freely. But more and more often, elephants are met by farms where humans grow crops elephants love to eat. Elephants accidentally destroy the farms, trying to get enough to eat. This leads to conflict, and all too often, death. Elephant populations are decreasing for these two key reasons.	Arash spoke rapidly without stopping to breathe: "But Ms. Soltys said that thousands of elephants are killed every year for their tusks, even though it's illegal! Plus, countries around the world have banned the selling of ivory!"

	Threats	Changes Needed
Declining Elephant Populations		
What a Mess!		
Stop Elephant Painting Now		

Name: _____ Date: _____

Directions: Closely read these paragraphs. Then, compare and contrast the ways in which people are trying to help elephants.

Close-Reading Texts

Elephants and Bees: One Solution	Stop Elephant Painting Now
First, King recorded the sound made by a hive of disturbed, angry bees. Then, she set up a sound system near a family of elephants resting in the shade of a tree. When King played the recording, the elephants' ears went up. Then, they started moving their heads from side to side. One elephant kicked a calf to get it up. Soon, they ran off! King repeated this experiment many times and found that 80 percent of the time, elephants avoided the bee noise. King's next step was to find farmers willing to build simple fences around their crops with beehives posted every 20 yards (18 meters). Her idea was that elephants would approach the farm and walk into the simple fence's wire. Then, the jiggling wire would wake up the bees, sending the elephants running. King tested her idea, and it worked! Today, dozens of farms are protected by these peacekeeping bees. These farms are in 19 countries, and the farmers are able to protect their crops and make money by selling the honey from the hives.	The next time you see a cute elephant painting a picture with its trunk, take a look at who's close by and what they are holding. If a trainer has a tool with a point or a hook on the end, the elephant is being trained to paint using methods that hurt the animal. This device is called a *bullhook*, and it is used in some American zoos and preserves to train elephants to do tricks. This barbaric device has been prohibited in some cities, but many more still use it. There are many reasons why these should be banned. First, elephants are not meant to do our bidding! Elephants are wild animals, and they do not paint for fun. They are not expressing their creativity by painting because are not naturally creative. In fact, they are trained to draw, and they need to be coaxed by trainers to produce (usually) the same painting every time! True sanctuaries for elephants don't force them to do tricks. Ban bullhooks now! Stop elephants from performing tricks! Sign the petition on the next page to help us save the elephants!

Elephants and Bees: One Solution   Stop Elephant Painting Now

135158—180 Days of Reading   © Shell Education

Directions: Think about the texts from this unit. Then, respond to the prompt.

Write a poem as an ode to the elephants. Consider the reasons why elephants are remarkable and worthy of adoration. Also include information about the threats to elephants to encourage your readers to take action.

_____
_____
_____
_____
_____
_____
_____
_____
_____
_____
_____
_____
_____
_____
_____
_____
_____
_____
_____
_____
_____
_____
_____
_____
_____
_____

Name: _____ **Date:** _____

Directions: Select an endangered animal to research. Identify actions that ordinary people can take to help protect this animal. Create an informative, persuasive poster to encourage people to take these actions.

My Animal: _____

Name: _____ **Date:** _____

Directions: Read the text, and answer the questions.

As You Read
Circle every mention of a specific time period.

An Old, Beloved Dessert

"I scream, you scream, we all scream for ice cream!" This classic rhyme still rings true today. Many people turn to a pint of ice cream to celebrate a special occasion or lift their spirits after a tough loss. In fact, it's estimated the average American enjoys about 20 pounds (9 kilograms) of ice cream every year!

Ice cream is one of the world's oldest desserts. It has likely been around, in various shapes or forms, for centuries. However, historians do not know who invented ice cream or where it originally came from. But here are some glimpses at its history. In China's T'ang period, emperors ate a frozen treat made with milk and flour. Around the 11th century, Persians had a recipe for an iced drink called *sharbat*. Iced desserts began to take off in Europe in the 17th century. Chefs started adding sugar to iced drinks, turning them into desserts. In 1686, Francesco Procopio opened a café in Paris. The café served ices and sherbets in tiny cups. These desserts of the past show us what the history of ice cream looked like. They also show how popular the beloved treat has remained through time!

1. Which is the best alternative title for this passage?
   - (A) Americans Love Ice Cream
   - (B) Chinese Invent Ice Cream
   - (C) The Mysterious Origins of Ice Cream
   - (D) Types of Dessert

2. Which of these events happened first?
   - (A) Persians had a drink called sharbat.
   - (B) Americans eat an average of 20 pounds of ice cream per year.
   - (C) Francesco Procopio opened a café in Paris.
   - (D) Iced desserts became popular in Europe.

3. Which is closest to the meaning of the idiom *still rings true* as it is used in the passage?
   - (A) is popular
   - (B) is accurate
   - (C) is catchy
   - (D) is new

4. What kind of sentence is this? *Many people turn to a pint of ice cream to celebrate a special occasion or lift their spirits after a tough loss.*
   - (A) simple
   - (B) compound
   - (C) complex
   - (D) compound-complex

5. Which is closest to the meaning of the phrase *take off* as it is used in the passage?
   - (A) lift off
   - (B) fly away
   - (C) become popular
   - (D) leave

6. Which of these words is **not** used to describe ice cream in this passage?
   - (A) treat
   - (B) beloved
   - (C) expensive
   - (D) frozen

Name: _____ **Date:** _____

Directions: Read the text, and answer the questions.

As You Read
Circle every mention of a specific time period.

American Arrival

In the 18th century, ice cream made its way to North America. European settlers sailed over, packing recipes for ice cream. In 1790, New York became home to the first ice cream parlor. The sweet, icy treat gained a famous fanbase among the wealthy. It was also popular with U.S. presidents. Records show that, one summer, President George Washington spent around $200 on ice cream! Thomas Jefferson and Dolley Madison also served ice cream to their guests.

For a long time, ice cream was a rare, expensive treat. It needed a cold environment to keep its shape. This was hard to do before the invention of refrigerators. And before the invention of electric equipment, making ice cream also took a lot of time and effort. Once these machines were created, ice cream became more accessible.

In the 1930s, people started to see ice cream on grocery store shelves. During World War II, ice cream's popularity soared. The sweet treat became a morale booster and symbol for the United States. Different military branches served ice cream to their troops to keep their spirits up. Since then, ice cream has been a dessert staple across the United States.

1. Which is a good synonym for the word *fanbase*?
   - (A) creators
   - (B) devotees
   - (C) observers
   - (D) nickname

2. Which line provides the best evidence that ice cream was enjoyed by some of the most famous people in early America?
   - (A) In the 18th century, ice cream made its way to North America.
   - (B) The sweet treat became a morale booster and symbol for the United States.
   - (C) European settlers sailed over, packing recipes for ice cream.
   - (D) Thomas Jefferson and Dolley Madison also served ice cream to their guests.

3. Why was ice cream expensive for so long?
   - (A) There were no refrigerators or freezers.
   - (B) The ingredients were rare.
   - (C) The sellers wanted to get rich.
   - (D) The equipment was expensive.

4. Which line from the text provides the best evidence that ice cream helped boost morale during World War II?
   - (A) And before the invention of electric equipment, making ice cream also took a lot of time and effort.
   - (B) Since then, ice cream has been a dessert staple across the United States.
   - (C) Different military branches served ice cream to their troops to keep their spirits up.
   - (D) Once these machines were created, ice cream became more accessible.

5. Which is a good synonym for *accessible* as it is used in this text?
   - (A) obtainable
   - (B) nearby
   - (C) obscure
   - (D) welcoming

6. What does *staple* mean in the phrase *a dessert staple*?
   - (A) unpopular
   - (B) frequently used
   - (C) rare
   - (D) new

Name: _____   **Date:** _____

Directions: Read the text, and answer the questions.

As You Read

Underline each ice cream flavor that is mentioned. Draw stars next to the ones you like.

Flavor Profiles

Why is ice cream so popular now and across history? For many people, the sweet treat is delicious and delightful. It is likely that part of ice cream's appeal is the variety; it comes in so many different flavors! Chefs across the world use their imaginations to dream up new flavor profiles, and no matter your preference, there is likely an ice cream flavor you will enjoy.

For starters, there are some classic ice cream flavors that have stood the test of time. In the United States, most ice cream eaters pick chocolate as their top flavor. Cookies 'n cream and vanilla also top the ice cream flavor charts. Strawberry, chocolate chip, and cookie dough are also fan favorites.

Ice cream flavors can also come with creative flair. Some inventive flavors include chile lime mango and lemon poppy seed! Ice cream is often served as a classic, comforting dessert, but the sweet treat can also experience a creative spin.

1. What literary device is used in this sentence? *For many people, the sweet treat is delicious and delightful.*
   - (A) metaphor
   - (B) hyperbole
   - (C) onomatopoeia
   - (D) alliteration

2. What kind of clause is this? *...but the sweet treat can also experience a creative spin.*
   - (A) dependent
   - (B) independent

3. What is the most popular ice cream flavor in the United States?
   - (A) vanilla
   - (B) chocolate
   - (C) strawberry
   - (D) cookies 'n cream

4. Which is a good synonym for the word *flair* as it is used in this text?
   - (A) pizzazz
   - (B) bounce
   - (C) similarity
   - (D) attempt

5. What is the main idea of this passage?

   _____

   _____

6. Do you like to try new and unusual ice cream flavors? What is the best flavor you have ever tried?

   _____

   _____

   _____

   _____

As You Read
Underline any words or processes that are new to you.

How to Make Ice Cream

Ice cream is made in vast quantities across the United States. Factories that make ice cream on a commercial level tend to follow the same process. They use heavy-duty machinery to make ice cream. Making ice cream at home looks a little bit different. Despite the differences in process, the results are the same—delicious ice cream!

At a factory, the first step in making ice cream starts with an ice cream mix. Factories create their own mix in a large vat. They start by adding liquid ingredients, such as cream, milk, and sugar syrups. The mix is stirred constantly while a computer controls the added amount of each ingredient. Dry ingredients are added next. These may include sugar, dried eggs, and stabilizers. Stabilizers help prevent ice crystals from forming in the ice cream.

When the ice cream mix is ready, the mix needs to be pasteurized and homogenized. Pasteurization occurs when something is heated to destroy harmful bacteria. Homogenization involves treating a product, such as milk, so that the fats are blended through the entire mix. Without this important step, the fats would separate and float to the top.

Next, the mix is left to settle for four to eight hours so the ingredients combine properly. Different flavorings are added to the mix to give the ice cream its unique flavor. Fruit, chocolate, nuts, or other solids are mixed in afterwards. In a factory, massive paddles churn in both the flavorings and solid additions.

Once the mix is flavored, it needs to be frozen and blended very quickly. The mix is pushed through a machine that freezes the mix while a blade blends it at the same time. The blade turns and whips the mix quickly, which adds air, giving ice cream its specific structure. Then, the ice cream is poured into containers. Ice cream is usually put into freezers to harden further because it has to be chilled to a low temperature for consumption.

Making ice cream at home is much simpler than making ice cream at a factory. If you are interested, start by researching "no-churn" methods for making ice cream. One of the most common methods is referred to as *ice cream in a bag*. A person makes an ice cream mix, pours the mix into a bag, and chills the bag until they're ready to continue. Then, they find a container with a lid. They fill the container with ice and salt, place the bag of ice cream mix inside, and put the lid on. Finally, they shake the container vigorously. After about 15 minutes, they have tasty ice cream.

Just like there are many ice cream flavors, there are many ways to make ice cream, too! No matter which method is used, the ice cream that is created is a delicious result.

Name: _____ **Date:** _____

Directions: Read "How to Make Ice Cream." Then, answer the questions.

1. What is the process by which any harmful bacteria are removed from the ice cream mix?

   Ⓐ homogenization
   Ⓑ pasteurization
   Ⓒ chilling
   Ⓓ ripening

2. When are flavorings added to the ice cream mix?

   Ⓐ after homogenization
   Ⓑ before pasteurization
   Ⓒ after being poured into containers
   Ⓓ before dry ingredients are added

3. True or false? It's impossible to make ice cream without special equipment.

   Ⓐ true
   Ⓑ false

4. Why is the ice cream stirred quickly?

   Ⓐ to make sure flavors are distributed
   Ⓑ to save time
   Ⓒ to add air to the mixture
   Ⓓ to distribute the fats

5. Which is a synonym for *consumption* as it is used in paragraph 5?

   Ⓐ ingestion   Ⓒ purchasing
   Ⓑ assimilation   Ⓓ sickness

6. What happens if you don't homogenize the mixture?

   Ⓐ Harmful bacteria can multiply.
   Ⓑ The fats separate and float to the top.
   Ⓒ Flavors are not mixed well.
   Ⓓ The ice cream will not have enough structure.

7. Use the text to complete the graphic organizer describing different ways to make ice cream.

Location	Ingredients	Equipment
Factory		
At Home		

Name: _____ **Date:** _____

Directions: Reread "How to Make Ice Cream." Then, respond to the prompt.

Invent a new ice cream flavor. Explain why it is the best flavor. Then, give step-by-step directions on how to make it at home.

_____
_____
_____
_____
_____
_____
_____
_____
_____
_____
_____
_____
_____
_____
_____
_____
_____
_____
_____
_____
_____
_____
_____
_____

Directions: Read the text, and answer the questions.

The Ice Cream War

It's Saturday at the town's weekly farmers market, and green tea gelato is running down my favorite white t-shirt. Asahi is standing across from me, wearing a fierce frown, his hands clenched in fists at his side. Asahi has been my best friend for three years running, but it's possible we're never, ever going to be friends again.

Let's rewind this story and start at the beginning, though. My name is Isabella, but everyone calls me Izzie (except my dad), and the most important fact about me is that I'm a complete nerd about ice cream. I know all the facts and figures behind how to make the world's best frozen treat. I can quote you the ingredients for vegan ice cream, what flavors of gelato are topping the charts, and I even know some of the big names throughout ice cream's history. For instance, I'll bet you have never heard of Augustus Jackson. He's nicknamed the "Father of Ice Cream." He didn't invent ice cream, but he came up with inventive ways to make it. He was one of the first chefs to make ice cream without eggs, and he used salt instead! No one else in my grade knows about Augustus Jackson—except Asahi.

1. Which word best describes the mood at the start of this story?
   - (A) friendly
   - (B) strained
   - (C) excited
   - (D) peaceful

2. Which is the best synonym for *nerd* as it is used in this text?
   - (A) bore
   - (B) drip
   - (C) connoisseur
   - (D) scientist

3. What form of figurative language is used in this sentence? *Asahi is standing across from me, wearing a fierce frown.*
   - (A) alliteration
   - (B) hyperbole
   - (C) rhyming
   - (D) repetition

4. Which word best describes Izzie's attitude toward ice cream?
   - (A) uninterested
   - (B) trepidation
   - (C) attention
   - (D) zealous

5. What do Izzie and Asahi share?
   - (A) all their classes
   - (B) a passion for the same interest
   - (C) the same neighborhood
   - (D) a medical condition

6. What literary device is introduced by this sentence? *Let's rewind this story and start at the beginning, though.*
   - (A) characterization
   - (B) flashback
   - (C) idiom
   - (D) imagery

Name: _____ Date: _____

Directions: Read the text, and answer the questions.

Let's Talk Ice Cream

I grew up trailing my dad around the kitchen, always asking him questions about what he was making. My dad runs our town's local ice cream shop. I love telling everyone I meet that he makes the best ice cream across 10 states. His shop uses a commercial ice cream maker, but he's also shown me how to whip ice cream into shape and how to use a bag to make our favorite sweet treat.

"What I love most about ice cream is how much creativity it demands," he told me once. "My ice cream flavors will always include vanilla and chocolate, of course. But how about ginger pineapple or cinnamon basil, too? There's such a range of flavor possibilities!"

I love chatting to people about ice cream, but sometimes I get the sense that people are, *maybe*, a little less interested. You know when you're looking at someone and their eyes start to glaze over as you're talking? Yeah, I've been there a time or two. But three years ago, I met Asahi, my first fellow ice cream aficionado.

1. What is Izzie's dad's favorite thing about ice cream?

- (A) the creaminess
- (B) original flavors
- (C) the cool temperature
- (D) the texture

2. What does it mean when someone's eyes "glaze over"?

- (A) They are excited.
- (B) They are feeling sentimental.
- (C) They are bored.
- (D) They are upset.

3. What is the tone of this sentence? *I love chatting to people about ice cream, but sometimes I get the sense that people are, maybe, a little less interested.*

- (A) sarcastic
- (B) irritated
- (C) resentful
- (D) objective

4. What kind of sentence is this? *I grew up trailing my dad around the kitchen, always asking him questions about what he was making.*

- (A) simple
- (B) compound
- (C) complex
- (D) compound-complex

5. What do Izzie and her father have in common?

- (A) They both love ice cream.
- (B) They both make ice cream.
- (C) They are both enthusiastic.
- (D) all of the above

6. Why was meeting Asahi so important to Izzie?

- (A) She had no other friends.
- (B) He was always kind to her.
- (C) He shares her passion.
- (D) She was bored.

Name: _____ **Date:** _____

Directions: Read the text, and answer the questions.

As You Read

Circle words and phrases that show Asahi's excitement about ice cream.

Izzie and Asahi

When Asahi and I first met, it was like meeting a long-lost friend. Asahi loves ice cream with the same fierceness that I do. Asahi grew up in Tokyo, so he grew up with a very different experience of ice cream. In our first conversation, he told me his favorite treat was mochi ice cream.

"Mochi are small, chewy rice cakes. Inside them, we sometimes put dollops of ice cream," Asahi said. Picturing a new form of ice cream, one I'd never heard of in all my research, boggled my mind! He smiled at my expression and invited me over to his house to try some.

Over the years, Asahi and I traded ice cream facts and experiences, and I often pulled him into my dad's kitchen. I loved showing Asahi how my dad experimented with different flavors, always trying to surprise his customers. Asahi looked at my dad in awe.

"You are like a chef *and* a scientist!" Asahi told him once. My dad laughed and laughed, and I had never felt so proud and seen because Asahi truly understood me and my family.

But everything changed when Asahi and his mom showed up at the farmers market with taiyaki ice cream.

1. How is mochi ice cream different from the ice cream in Izzie's dad's shop?
   - (A) It is not sweet.
   - (B) It is covered in rice cakes.
   - (C) It is served only in cones.
   - (D) It has only one flavor.

2. What is the meaning for *boggled* as it is used in the text?
   - (A) impressed
   - (B) confident
   - (C) perplexed
   - (D) amused

3. In what way does Asahi view Izzie's dad like a scientist?
   - (A) He uses chemicals.
   - (B) He has a Ph.D.
   - (C) He experiments with new flavors.
   - (D) He wears safety goggles.

4. What does Izzie mean in the fourth paragraph when she says that she felt *seen*?
   - (A) Asahi compliments her on her clothes.
   - (B) Asahi is a good listener.
   - (C) Asahi shares a lot about himself.
   - (D) Asahi understands her.

5. What do you predict will happen at the farmers market?

   _____

   _____

   _____

As You Read

Underline the events that cause the conflict. Then, star the events that resolve it.

Enough for All

For my whole life, the farmers market has run on Saturdays, rain or shine. My dad has always had a stand at the southeast corner, and that is where we sell our pints of ice cream. We bring the shop's top five flavors, and it's my favorite thing in the world to help my dad out on Saturdays. Our stand always has a massive line, and we have regulars that come every week for a pint of my dad's famous French vanilla ice cream. But this week, our stand is missing its usual line of customers.

"No one's coming here," I say, "so maybe we should go around handing out flyers?"

My dad shrugs and says, "Most people are probably checking out the Tanakas' taiyaki ice cream booth."

I can already feel the disbelief curdling in my stomach. "Asahi's family is selling ice cream here at the market?"

My dad frowns and tells me he thought I knew, but I'm already marching away in search of Asahi. I see him with his mom, handing out taiyaki ice cream. He told me once that they were grilled cakes shaped like fish, and some people in the United States use them as cones and put ice cream inside. Now, there he is, handing out taiyaki ice cream to all my dad's customers!

I stomp over to Asahi and pull a taiyaki ice cream from his hands before he can hand it out. Asahi startles in surprise, his arm pushing outward, and I stagger backwards, feeling a cold splash on my white t-shirt. As I look down, there are rivers of green tea gelato pouring down my shirt and a taiyaki cone at my feet. When I look up, Asahi is glaring at me, and I regret my impulsive move.

"I am so, so sorry, Asahi," I start, and Asahi's frown quickly fades as he lowers his head. "But how could you not tell me you and your mom were selling ice cream at the farmers market?"

Asahi pulls me to the side, and he says, "You are so proud of what your family has built in this town, but my family also loves ice cream and sharing what we make with others. I promise, we talked to your dad before setting up our own booth at the market, and he told us there was 'enough for all.'"

My dad is always telling me there is "enough for all" and that we should believe in abundance. I reach out my hand to Asahi, and I take a deep breath.

"I wish you had told me, but I understand now. Welcome to the market, Asahi."

The two of us smile at each other, tentatively, and Asahi hands me a fresh taiyaki cone.

Name: _____ **Date:** _____

Directions: Read "Enough for All." Then, answer the questions.

1. Why does Izzie's dad's stand have fewer customers than usual?
   - (A) The farmers market is less crowded in general.
   - (B) He didn't bring any popular flavors.
   - (C) The weather is not good.
   - (D) People want to try the taiyaka ice cream.

2. How does Izzie feel when she hears about what Asahi's family is doing?
   - (A) unconcerned
   - (B) surprised and angry
   - (C) surprised and excited
   - (D) saddened

3. Which of these words is used as an adverb in the text?
   - (A) regulars
   - (B) tentatively
   - (C) stagger
   - (D) feeling

4. What is Izzie's father advocating for when he says there is "enough for all"?
   - (A) planning ahead
   - (B) curiosity
   - (C) generosity
   - (D) simplicity

5. How does Izzie feel at the end of the story?
   - (A) remorseful
   - (B) joyful
   - (C) worried
   - (D) jealous

6. What literary device does the author employ in this phrase? *…there are rivers of green tea gelato pouring down my shirt…*
   - (A) simile
   - (B) imagery
   - (C) personification
   - (D) onomatopoeia

7. Summarize the conflict, its causes, and the solution in the chart.

Conflict	Causes of Conflict	Solution

Directions: Reread "Enough for All." Then, respond to the prompt.

Rewrite the ending of the story from Asahi's perspective. Feel free to change the outcome if you would like.

_____
_____
_____
_____
_____
_____
_____
_____
_____
_____
_____
_____
_____
_____
_____
_____
_____
_____
_____
_____
_____
_____
_____
_____

BANANA ICE CREAM

Did you know you can make ice cream with just one ingredient? That's right, this one-ingredient ice cream recipe calls for just four frozen bananas!

INGREDIENTS

- 4 bananas
- *optional:* 3 tablespoons of dairy milk, almond milk, or any milk of your choice
- *optional:* peanut butter, honey, or chocolate chips to add on top

EQUIPMENT NEEDED

- freezer bag
- freezer
- blender
- *optional:* container

DIRECTIONS

1. Select four ripe bananas.
2. Peel the bananas, and cut them into small pieces.
3. Put the banana pieces into a freezer bag. Place the bag in a freezer for at least six hours.
4. Take out the frozen banana pieces, and blend them together in a blender. You can add a few tablespoons of milk to the mixture, if desired. Blend until smooth.
5. Serve now or put the ice cream in a container and freeze it for another two hours.
6. Scoop and enjoy! You can choose to add peanut butter, honey, or chocolate chips on top.

Directions: Read "Banana Ice Cream." Then, answer the questions.

1. What can you infer from the introduction to the recipe?

   Ⓐ Most people love bananas.

   Ⓑ Most people have never made their own ice cream.

   Ⓒ Most ice cream recipes have multiple ingredients.

   Ⓓ Most people have bananas in their freezers.

2. Which of these steps occurs first?

   Ⓐ adding chocolate chips

   Ⓑ cutting the bananas

   Ⓒ freezing the bananas

   Ⓓ blending the bananas

3. Which is a synonym for *optional*?

   Ⓐ elective   Ⓒ obligatory

   Ⓑ compulsory   Ⓓ candidacy

4. True or false? All ice cream has dairy in it.

   Ⓐ true

   Ⓑ false

5. What kind of sentence is this? *Take out the frozen banana pieces, and blend them together in a blender.*

   Ⓐ simple

   Ⓑ compound

   Ⓒ complex

   Ⓓ compound-complex

6. What does the adjective *smooth* modify in this sentence? *Blend until smooth.*

   Ⓐ make

   Ⓑ mixture

   Ⓒ melded

   Ⓓ until

7. Record at least 10 nouns, verbs, and adjectives from the recipe.

Nouns	Verbs	Adjectives

Name: _____ **Date:** _____

Directions: Closely read these paragraphs. Then, reread the recipe on page 77. Examine the range of ingredients and flavors that are described. Record the information in the chart.

Close-Reading Texts

Flavor Profiles	Izzie and Asahi
For starters, there are some classic ice cream flavors that have stood the test of time. In the United States, most ice cream eaters pick chocolate as their top flavor. Cookies n' cream and vanilla also top the ice cream flavor charts. Strawberry, chocolate chip, and cookie dough are also fan favorites. Ice cream flavors can also come with creative flair. Some inventive flavors include chile lime mango and lemon poppy seed! Ice cream is often served as a classic, comforting dessert, but the sweet treat can also experience a creative spin.	Asahi grew up in Tokyo, so he grew up with a very different experience of ice cream. In our first conversation, he told me his favorite treat was mochi ice cream. "Mochi are small, chewy rice cakes. Inside them, we sometimes put dollops of ice cream," Asahi said. Picturing a new form of ice cream, one I'd never heard of in all my research, boggled my mind! He smiled at my expression and invited me over to his house to try some.

Text	Ingredients and Flavors
Flavor Profiles	
Izzie and Asahi	
Banana Ice Cream	

Name: _____ Date: _____

Directions: Closely read these paragraphs. Then, compare and contrast the process of making ice cream in the 18th century and today.

Close-Reading Texts

18th Century: American Arrival

European settlers sailed over, packing recipes for ice cream. In 1790, New York became home to the first ice cream parlor. The sweet, icy treat gained a famous fanbase among the wealthy. It was also popular with U.S. presidents. Records show that, one summer, President George Washington spent around $200 on ice cream! Thomas Jefferson and Dolley Madison also served ice cream to their guests.

For a long time, ice cream was a rare, expensive treat. It needed a cold environment to keep its shape. This was hard to do before the invention of refrigerators. And before the invention of electric equipment, making ice cream also took a lot of time and effort. Once these machines were created, ice cream became more accessible.

Today: How to Make Ice Cream

Factories create their own mix in a large vat. They start by adding liquid ingredients, such as cream, milk, and sugar syrups. The mix is stirred constantly while a computer controls the added amount of each ingredient. Dry ingredients are added next. These may include sugar, dried eggs, and stabilizers. Stabilizers help prevent ice crystals from forming in the ice cream.

When the ice cream mix is ready, the mix needs to be pasteurized and homogenized...

Next, the mix is left to settle for four to six hours so the ingredients combine properly. Different flavorings are added to the mix to give the ice cream its unique flavor...

Once the mix is flavored, it needs to be frozen and blended very quickly...Then, the ice cream is poured into containers.

18th Century	Today

Both

Name: _____ **Date:** _____

Directions: Think about the texts from this unit. Then, respond to the prompt.

You and your family can only eat one specific dessert for the rest of your life. You will vote after hearing an argument in favor of each choice. Write a speech explaining your choice and why it is the best possible choice. Use persuasive language, and explain why other possible choices would be inferior.

_____
_____
_____
_____
_____
_____
_____
_____
_____
_____
_____
_____
_____
_____
_____
_____
_____
_____
_____
_____
_____
_____

Name: _____ Date: _____

Directions: Reread "Banana Ice Cream." Think about your favorite food. If you don't already know how to make it, research recipes. Then, record a simplified form of your recipe.

My Favorite _____

Ingredients

_____

_____

_____

_____

_____

_____

_____

_____

Equipment

_____

_____

_____

_____

_____

_____

_____

Steps

_____

_____

_____

_____

_____

_____

_____

_____

_____

_____

_____

_____

_____

_____

Name: _____ **Date:** _____

Directions: Read the text, and answer the questions.

As You Read
Underline inaccurate beliefs people have about pirates.

Talk Like a Pirate Day

In 1995, John Baur and Mark Summers of Albany, Oregon, came up with a new holiday. They decided that September 19 would forever be known as Talk Like a Pirate Day. To celebrate, you just have to talk like a pirate! There are a few popular noises and phrases people say when they pretend to be pirates. You might hear someone yell, "Arrrr!" Another popular phrase is "Shiver me timbers." And if someone upsets you, you can always call them a "scallywag."

In reality, pirates never talked this way! They also did not dress like the pirates you may have seen in movies or cartoons. They did not wear eye patches or lots of earrings. In fact, many of the stereotypes about pirates come from a movie made in the 1950s called *Treasure Island*. The star actor, Robert Newton, used an exaggerated English accent for the role. His accent has become synonymous with pirate talk, even though pirates came from all over the world. They were not always as lawless and fearsome as they were made out to be. Some pirates had families, went to church, and otherwise contributed to their communities.

1. True or false? Pirates are accurately portrayed in movies.
   - (A) true
   - (B) false

2. Where do many of our ideas about pirates come from originally?
   - (A) Talk Like a Pirate Day
   - (B) history books
   - (C) comic books
   - (D) *Treasure Island*

3. What literary device is used in the phrase *people pretending to be pirates*?
   - (A) hyperbole
   - (B) alliteration
   - (C) metaphor
   - (D) simile

4. Which is the best synonym for *stereotypes* as it is used in the text?
   - (A) ideas
   - (B) examples
   - (C) differences
   - (D) clichés

5. Which word best describes the author's attitude toward pirates?
   - (A) neutral
   - (B) admiring
   - (C) negative
   - (D) conflicted

6. What is the author's purpose in writing this text?
   - (A) to challenge misinformation
   - (B) to repeat well-known facts
   - (C) to persuade
   - (D) to encourage

Name: _____ Date: _____

Directions: Read the text, and answer the questions.

As You Read
Underline inaccurate beliefs people have about pirates.

Pirate Myths

The blindfolded sailor slowly and bravely stepped onto the plank, prodded on by the tip of the pirate captain's sword. His fate awaited him in the rushing water below.

The text above may sound like typical pirate actions, but it never happened! Pirates didn't make people walk the plank because their ships didn't have planks. Also, even though some pirates may have lost arms and legs and replaced them with wooden pegs and hooks, this was most likely a rare occurrence. The same was true for missing eyes and eye patches.

One of the most popular pirate myths is that pirates buried their treasure and would go back to get it. Legend says that Blackbeard, one of history's most famous pirates, buried large amounts of treasure. When the wreck of Blackbeard's ship, *Queen Anne's Revenge*, was found in the 1990s, divers did not find treasure on it. Instead of treasure, divers found navigational devices, books, cannons, and a sword hilt. To this day, no one has ever found treasure that Blackbeard buried. So, in reality, burying and finding treasure didn't happen. Piracy was more about stealing goods from ships rather than searching for buried gold and treasure.

1. The clause *prodded on by the tip of the captain's sword* from the first sentence is an example of a/an _____ clause.
   - (A) dependent
   - (B) independent

2. Which of these is **not** a myth about pirates?
   - (A) They were violent.
   - (B) They wore eye patches.
   - (C) They buried treasure.
   - (D) They made people walk the plank.

3. Which is a synonym for *myth*?
   - (A) fact
   - (B) information
   - (C) allegory
   - (D) legend

4. Which word best describes how pirates are depicted in common myths?
   - (A) kind
   - (B) ruthless
   - (C) selfless
   - (D) healthy

5. What kind of items were found in Blackbeard's shipwreck?
   - (A) his treasure chest
   - (B) items used in sailing and fighting
   - (C) valuable items to sell in Europe
   - (D) gold and other natural resources

6. Which of the following is a compound sentence?
   - (A) The same was true for missing eyes and eye patches.
   - (B) To this day, no one has ever found treasure that Blackbeard buried.
   - (C) Pirates didn't make people walk the plank because their ships didn't have planks.
   - (D) Sounds like typical pirate stuff, but it never happened!

Directions: Read the text, and answer the questions.

As You Read

Circle all the verbs that show what Shih Yang did in her life.

No Women Allowed

One thing most pirates (and other sailors) of yore could agree on was that having a woman aboard was bad luck. At the time, captains believed that a woman's presence could anger the sea gods or cause storms and waves. However, these beliefs did not keep some women from boarding ships! There are even a few stories of women thieving and pillaging along with their male counterparts.

Shih Yang is one example of a woman who braved the seas as a pirate. She grew up in Southern China in the late 1700s. When she was captured by pirates at the age of 15, they enslaved her and forced her to work on the ship. She was clever, though, and as she worked, she listened and learned many of the pirates' secrets. Shih Yang married a pirate, and together they commanded the Red Flag Fleet, which was a fierce pirate army that had almost 50,000 members. When her husband died, she took over the fleet by herself. One of her most important laws was that female pirates in her fleet had to be treated with respect. After 10 years commanding the seas, Shih Yang retired to a quiet life with her family.

1. What is the meaning of *yore* as used in the text?

- (A) belonging to you
- (B) China
- (C) the sea
- (D) a long time ago

2. What does the word *these* refer to in the third sentence?

- (A) angry sea gods
- (B) beliefs about women
- (C) lack of ship experience
- (D) weakness

3. Which of these events happened third?

- (A) Shih Yang married a pirate.
- (B) Shih Yang was captured by pirates.
- (C) Shih Yang lived a quiet life with her children.
- (D) Shih Yang commanded the Red Flag Fleet.

4. What is the main idea of this passage?

_____

_____

_____

5. Why do you think Shih Yang retired from being a pirate commander after 10 years?

_____

_____

_____

As You Read
Underline every physical description of Blackbeard.

Blackbeard's Bad Reputation

Imagine that your ship is racing as fast as it can across the Atlantic. But the *Queen Anne's Revenge*, the most terrifying pirate ship on the seas, is getting closer. Finally, it pulls up beside you, and its cannons are aimed and ready to fire. Out of the shadows of the deck appears a tall man with broad shoulders, a wide hat, and a long, black beard. Around his neck are three pistols, and smoke is coming from his head and beard. It's Blackbeard, the most infamous pirate to ever set sail! Blackbeard and his pirates round up your crewmates, keeping an eye on you while they ransack your ship. And on the day the most notorious pirate boards your ship, not only does no one die, no one even gets hurt. Blackbeard and his crew leaves when they are done, and you get to keep your ship!

Blackbeard is perhaps the best-known pirate of the golden age of piracy. This time period ranged from the late 1600s to the 1720s. One of the biggest myths surrounding Blackbeard is that he was a violent killer. But there is no evidence that Blackbeard ever hurt anyone as a pirate until his final battle. No matter what people think about pirates from this time, Blackbeard relied on his carefully created reputation instead of the cannons on his ship or the pistols around his neck. Tall tales told of his "wild eyes" and "murderous image." These fake myths worked a lot better than actual violence. It was also said that smoke came from his beard, and apparently, Blackbeard lit slow-burning matches and placed them in his beard to create the menacing smoke.

All myths aside, Blackbeard was not like the rumors and exaggerations made him out to be. First, he treated his crew favorably. He liked to read, and he was known to steal books from ships for his personal library. He also had a French chef on board his ship so he could provide good food for his crew. Ultimately, his habit of leaving his victims alive brought about his downfall.

On November 22, 1718, members of the British Navy sailed to the area where Blackbeard's ship was anchored and ambushed him. They were working off a tip they had received from a sea captain who had been released by Blackbeard. While Blackbeard didn't often use violence, he wasn't afraid to use weapons if he was forced to. Accounts of that day say that Blackbeard "stood his ground, and fought with great fury, till he received five and twenty wounds." Blackbeard had gotten many injuries, and he died after the battle.

Though Blackbeard may have been fearsome in people's minds throughout his life, in reality, he was not as violent as he seemed!

Name: _____ **Date:** _____

Directions: Read "Blackbeard's Bad Reputation." Then, answer the questions.

1. What was the *Queen Anne's Revenge*?

- (A) a story about pirates
- (B) a famous pirate ship
- (C) a law passed by Queen Anne
- (D) the site of Blackbeard's treasure

2. From what point of view is the first paragraph written?

- (A) first-person
- (B) second-person
- (C) third-person
- (D) first- and second-person

3. What was Blackbeard's most "powerful" weapon?

- (A) his cannons
- (B) his reputation
- (C) his character
- (D) his pistols

4. What do accounts of Blackbeard's death imply?

- (A) Blackbeard was a poor fighter.
- (B) Blackbeard was a coward.
- (C) Blackbeard kept fighting when injured.
- (D) Blackbeard refused to fight the British Navy.

5. Which pair of words have the same meaning?

- (A) *demise* and *fury*
- (B) *ransack* and *plunder*
- (C) *infamous* and *violent*
- (D) *notorious* and *murderous*

6. Write facts and myths about Blackbeard in the chart.

Facts	Myths

Name: _____ **Date:** _____

Directions: Reread "Blackbeard's Bad Reputation." Then, respond to the prompt.

Imagine you were on a ship captured by Blackbeard. Write an account of that day describing Blackbeard and how he treated you and your crew. How did you feel from beginning to end?

_____
_____
_____
_____
_____
_____
_____
_____
_____
_____
_____
_____
_____
_____
_____
_____
_____
_____
_____
_____
_____
_____
_____
_____
_____

Directions: Read the text, and answer the questions.

As You Read
Underline the key events in Anne's early life.

Anne with the Bright Red Hair

My name is Anne, and I was born around the year 1700 in County Cork, Ireland. I say "around" because my father, William Cormac, couldn't remember exactly which year I was born. He used to dress me in boy's clothing so that I could be taken on as an apprentice as a lawyer's clerk. Unfortunately, wherever my father went, trouble followed. We moved around a lot as I was growing up. Before I was 11 years old, we moved to London, and a few months later, we moved to the colonies overseas. We ultimately ended up in Charleston, South Carolina, which is where I became known as Anne with the bright red hair and matching bad temper. You may have heard the rumors that I stabbed someone at the tender age of 13. On that topic, let's just say that at that point in my life, I hadn't yet learned to wield a knife.

As opposed to many other pirates you may have heard of, I came from means. We lived in a townhouse, and my father made plenty of money as a merchant. Perhaps my life would have been quieter and easier if I hadn't met James Bonny.

1. What is the meaning of the phrase *came from means*?

- (A) came from Ireland
- (B) came from a wealthy family
- (C) was well-meaning
- (D) came with purpose

2. Why does the author imply with this statement? *Let's just say that at that point in my life, I hadn't yet learned to wield a knife.*

- (A) Anne was guilty of the stabbing at age 13.
- (B) Anne disliked using violence for any reason.
- (C) Anne eventually became comfortable with violence.
- (D) Anne preferred other weapons.

3. Which is a synonym for *apprentice*?

- (A) teacher
- (C) trainee
- (B) expert
- (D) child

4. Which literary device is this statement? *Perhaps my life would have been quieter and easier if I hadn't met James Bonny.*

- (A) simile
- (B) hyperbole
- (C) alliteration
- (D) foreshadowing

5. What can you infer about James Bonny?

- (A) He was a lawyer.
- (B) He caused trouble for Anne.
- (C) He and Anne moved back to Ireland.
- (D) He was a friend of Anne's father.

6. True or false? Few pirates came from wealthy families.

- (A) true
- (B) false

Name: _____   **Date:** _____

Directions: Read the text, and answer the questions.

As You Read
Circle words or phrases that describe how Anne views James over time.

James Bonny the Spy

James Bonny was a small-time pirate, and of course my father did not approve of him. But as it happened, I was in love, and nothing would alter my devotion to him. So, we hopped aboard a ship and sailed to the Bahamas, which was a sanctuary for pirates. James and I headed to the docks every morning looking for work and some fun. Pirates had always told grand tales of adventure, and I loved listening and wondering how a woman such as myself could have similar adventures.

One day, James came home with enough money to drag us out of poverty. When I asked him where he had gotten it, he replied that he had done a few odd jobs. I suspected he was not being truthful, so I followed him the next morning and found him conversing suspiciously with one of the governor's men. They whispered for a while, and then the man slipped James a silver coin. That's how I came to learn that my James was a snitch, and he was the one responsible for our pirate friends getting arrested. I could not stand for that, so I decided to use one of my father's tricks to get away.

1. Which of these statements is supported by the text?
- (A) James is not a successful pirate.
- (B) James and Anne are living comfortably.
- (C) Anne stays home while James works.
- (D) James and Anne fight frequently.

2. Why do James and Anne move to the Bahamas?
- (A) It has beautiful beaches.
- (B) It has good docks.
- (C) It is a safe place for pirates.
- (D) Anne's father is moving there.

3. Which is an antonym for *suspiciously*?
- (A) shadily
- (B) innocently
- (C) questionably
- (D) easily

4. Which of these events happens first?
- (A) James whispers with one of the governor's men.
- (B) Anne follows James.
- (C) James brings home a lot of money.
- (D) Anne decides to leave James.

5. What connotation does the word *snitch* have?
- (A) positive
- (B) negative
- (C) neutral

6. Why does Anne decide to get away?
- (A) She and James can no longer find work.
- (B) She wants to live somewhere else.
- (C) She is tired of not having enough money.
- (D) She is upset that James is a spy.

Directions: Read the text, and answer the questions.

As You Read
Underline all the dialogue.

A Big Surprise

Disguised as a man, I approached Calico Jack, a pirate captain who had docked his ship named *Revenge* for some needed repairs. I convinced him to take me on as a part of his crew, and we set sail a few days later. My life as a pirate began, and I learned to swab the deck and climb high to the crow's nest to search for ships to attack. I also learned how to use a cannon and a knife, which I must admit was quite thrilling.

Jack was able to discern my true nature pretty early on, but he promised to stay tight-lipped about it. I got along well with most of the crew and even earned their respect. I became good friends with the the lieutenant, Mark Reed, but keeping my secret from him became increasingly difficult. One day I decided to barge into his cabin, and I stated plainly, "Lieutenant Reed, I am a woman!"

"Well, that's quite a coincidence," Reed replied with a smirk.

"What makes it such a coincidence?" I asked, my temper rising quickly. Reed slowly removed his hat, and a long train of brown hair fell down his back.

"Well, my real name is Mary."

1. Which of her father's tricks does Anne employ?

   (A) She is being disloyal to her captain.

   (B) She is stealing from her ship.

   (C) She is disguising herself as man.

   (D) She is leaving for a new country.

2. Why does Reed respond with a smirk?

   (A) Reed is angry.

   (B) Reed is confused.

   (C) Reed is uninterested.

   (D) Reed is amused.

3. How did Calico Jack feel about Anne being a woman?

   (A) He never knew.

   (B) He did not care.

   (C) He thought it was funny.

   (D) He was annoyed.

4. How does Anne like being a pirate? Why?

   _____

   _____

5. Make a prediction. What will happen now that Mary and Anne know about each other? Why?

   _____

   _____

   _____

Name: _____   Date: _____

As You Read
Mark positive events with a plus sign and negative events with a minus sign.

Sisters of the Sea

If one woman aboard a pirate ship was supposed to bring bad luck, what did it mean to have two women on board? Mary and I decided to stop masquerading as men and simply went about our business as the women we were. Eventually, the men adjusted and accepted us, but it took some time. What helped is that we worked twice as hard as they did and could fight with the best of them. Plus, we had been reaping the riches of pirating. Bad luck had refused to rear its head, despite the superstitions. Mary and I helped attack ship after ship in the southern seas, gaining fortune and recognition with each successful haul.

As with all things, I suppose, our good luck was due to expire sooner or later. Sea captains began to bring home tales of a mysterious pirate ship with women who fought alongside the men. A British Navy ship was sent out to find us, and one fateful night, they caught up to us! Mary and I were on watch duty while the rest of the crew slept, and because we could not raise the sails by ourselves, we decided to stay and fight. I called to the crew in their sleeping quarters, but Calico Jack himself told us to give up the fight.

"If you cowards won't fight, then Mary and I will," I said, pushing poor old Jack back down the stairs and drawing my sword.

Mary and I fought off the British Navy by ourselves for the better part of an hour with bullets, knives, and swords until we were surrounded. Ultimately, we lay down our weapons and surrendered. We looked upon the faint-hearted pirates of our crew as we were escorted off our ship in chains.

All these events have brought me to today, the day of my trial. I miss my friend Mary desperately; she is not actually here with me because she took ill last week and was removed from our cell. I heard a rumor that she was able to recover and actually escaped, which is what I plan to do as well. I've already managed to get one hand out of my chains, and when I have my other hand free, I'll be able to fight off the guards when they come to get me. I'll change my name and explore the town until I find my dearest friend. Together, we'll have our own ship and do as we please, because we are sisters of the sea, and the pirate life is for us!

Directions: Read "Sisters of the Sea." Then, answer the questions.

1. Why do their fellow pirates accept Mary and Anne?

    (A) Mary and Anne were good pirates.

    (B) Mary and Anne were charming women.

    (C) Mary and Anne bullied them.

    (D) Mary and Anne were in charge.

2. What is supposed to happen on the final day of the story?

    (A) Anne's capture

    (B) Mary's discovery

    (C) Anne's trial

    (D) Mary's execution

3. Which is the best synonym for *expire* as it is used in paragraph 2?

    (A) rot   (C) increase

    (B) decease   (D) run out

4. What is an antonym for *faint-hearted*?

    (A) frightened   (C) loving

    (B) courageous (D) malicious

5. Which of these words best describes Anne?

    (A) kind   (C) fierce

    (B) positive   (D) tired

6. Identify and record evidence from the text that supports each of the following character traits for Anne.

Character Trait	Evidence from Text
Brave	
Persistent	
Confident	

Name: _____ **Date:** _____

Directions: Reread "Sisters of the Sea." Then, respond to the prompt.

Imagine that Mary and Anne are eventually reunited. Tell the story of what happened to either Anne or Mary in between the ending of the story on page 94 and their reunion.

_____

_____

_____

_____

_____

_____

_____

_____

_____

_____

_____

_____

_____

_____

_____

_____

_____

_____

_____

_____

_____

_____

_____

A SEA SHANTY

Sea shanties are folk songs originally sung by sailors while working on their ships. Most shanties were sung as call and response. One singer would sing the story, and the rest of the crew sang the chorus. High Barbary was a nickname of a coastline in North Africa. This was the home of the Barbary pirates from the 1500s until the 1800s. This is a transcript of an old sea shanty.

Text

Robertson, Sidney—collector
Graham, George Vinton—singer
Asmussen, Ella—transcriber of text

Recorded at San Jose, California
December 1938
UC-WPA Disk No. 4E-B1

Down Around the Coast of Les Barbarees *

Oh, its two gallant ships from England they did sail,
So high, so low, and so sail we;
It was one the Prince of Prussia and the other, Prince of Wales
Cruising around down the Coast of Les Barbarees.

"Jump aloft, jump aloft," our gallant captain cried,
So high, so low, and so sail we;
"Look ahead, look astern, look alarboard, look a-lee,
Look around down the Coast of Les Barbarees."

Oh, there's nothing ahead and there's nothing astern,
So high, so low, and so sail we;
But the wind is on the breakers and the lofty ship is seen
Cruising around down the Coast of Les Barbarees.
But the wind is on the breakers and the lofty ship is seen
Cruising around down the Coast of Les Barbarees.

"Oh, hail her, oh, hail her," the gallant captain cried,
So high, so low and so sail we;
"Are you a man of war or a privateer," said he,
"Cruising around down the Coast of Les Barbarees?"
"Are you a man of war or a privateer," said he,
"Cruising around down the Coast of Les Barbarees?"

"I'm not a man of war, nor a privateer," said he,
So high, so low and so sail we;
"But I am a sassy pirate and I'm waiting for my pay,
Cruising around down the Coast of Les Barbarees."
"But I am a sassy pirate and I'm waiting for my pay,
Cruising around down the Coast of Les Barbarees."

Then it's two-sided broad side these two lofty ships did pour,
So high, so low, and so sail we;
'Til at length the Prince of Prussia shot away the pirates' mast,
Cruising around down the Coast of Les Barbarees.

"Oh, for quarters, for quarters!" a saucy pirate cried,
So high, so low, and so sail we;
"But the quarters that we'll give you, we will sink you in the sea,
Cruising around down the Coast of Les Barbarees.
But the quarters that we'll give you, we will sink you in the sea.

* Mr. Graham's spelling in his MS. copy is La Barbaree, but he
pronounces it with a long "a".

Name: _____ **Date:** _____

Directions: Read "A Sea Shanty." Then, answer the questions.

1. What is the setting of the song?

  Ⓐ on land along the coast
  Ⓑ docked in England
  Ⓒ on ships off the coast of Africa
  Ⓓ on ships off the coast of England

2. Based on the text, what is the meaning of *transcript*?

  Ⓐ a spoken lyric
  Ⓑ a typed copy
  Ⓒ a way of listening
  Ⓓ a type of money

3. Which literary device is used in this song?

  Ⓐ personification
  Ⓑ hyperbole
  Ⓒ simile
  Ⓓ repetition

4. Based on the context, what is the likely meaning of *Oh, for quarters, for quarters!*

  Ⓐ Thank you!
  Ⓑ Good grief!
  Ⓒ Have mercy!
  Ⓓ You rascals!

5. What do you think is the author's purpose in writing this song, other than to entertain? Why?

_____
_____
_____
_____
_____
_____

Name: _____ Date: _____

Directions: Closely read these excerpts. Examine how the characters of Blackbeard and Anne are portrayed. Record the information in the chart.

Close-Reading Texts

Blackbeard's Bad Reputation	Sisters of the Sea
Out of the shadows of the deck appears a tall man with broad shoulders, a wide hat, and a long, black beard. Around his neck are three pistols, and smoke is coming from his head and beard. It's Blackbeard, the most infamous pirate to ever set sail! … No matter what people think about pirates from this time, Blackbeard relied on his carefully created reputation instead of the cannons on his ship or the pistols around his shoulder. Tall tales told of his "wild eyes" and "murderous image." These fake myths worked a lot better than actual violence. It was also said that smoke came from his beard, and apparently, Blackbeard lit slow-burning matches and placed them in his beard to create the menacing smoke.

All myths aside, Blackbeard was not like the rumors and exaggerations made him out to be. First, he treated his crew favorably. He liked to read, and he was known to steal books from ships for his personal library. He also had a French chef on board his ship so he could provide good food for his crew. Ultimately, his habit of leaving his victims alive brought about his downfall. | "If you cowards won't fight, then Mary and I will," I said, pushing poor old Jack back down the stairs and drawing my sword.

Mary and I fought off the British Navy by ourselves for the better part of an hour with bullets, knives, and swords until we were surrounded. Ultimately, we lay down our weapons and surrendered. We looked upon the faint-hearted pirates of our crew as we were escorted off our ship in chains.

All these events have brought me to today, the day of my trial. I miss my friend Mary desperately; she is not actually here with me because she took ill last week and was removed from our cell. I heard a rumor that she was able to recover and actually escaped, which is what I plan to do as well. I've already managed to get one hand out of my chains, and when I have my other hand free, I'll be able to fight off the guards when they come to get me. I'll change my name and explore the town until I find my dearest friend. Together, we'll have our own ship and do as we please, because we are sisters of the sea, and the pirate life is for us! |

	Character Description	**Why They Are Successful Pirates**
Blackbeard's Bad Reputation		
Sisters of the Sea		

Name: _____ Date: _____

Directions: Closely read the excerpts. Then, compare and contrast the way that women pirates are depicted in each account.

Close-Reading Texts

No Women Allowed	Sisters of the Sea
One thing most pirates (and other sailors) of yore could agree on was that having a woman aboard was bad luck. At the time, captains believed that a woman's presence could anger the sea gods or cause storms and waves. However, these beliefs did not keep some women from boarding ships! There are even a few stories of women thieving and pillaging along with their male counterparts. Shih Yang is one example of a woman who braved the seas as a pirate. She grew up in Southern China in the late 1700s. When she was captured by pirates at the age of 15, they enslaved her and forced her to work on the ship. She was clever, though, and as she worked, she listened and learned many of the pirates' secrets. Shih Yang married a pirate, and together they commanded the Red Flag Fleet, which was a fierce pirate army that had almost 50,000 members. When her husband died, she took over the fleet by herself. One of her most important laws was that female pirates in her fleet had to be treated with respect. After 10 years commanding the seas, Shih Yang retired to a quiet life with her family.	If one woman aboard a pirate ship was supposed to bring bad luck, what did it mean to have two women on board? Mary and I decided to stop masquerading as men and simply went about our business as the women we were. Eventually, the men adjusted and accepted us, but it took some time. What helped is that we worked twice as hard as they did and could fight with the best of them. Plus, we had been reaping the riches of pirating. Bad luck had refused to rear its head, despite the superstitions. Mary and I helped attack ship after ship in the southern seas, gaining fortune and recognition with each successful haul.

No Women Allowed	Sisters of the Sea

Both

Name: _____ **Date:** _____

Directions: Think about the texts from this unit. Then, respond to the prompt.

Consider all you have learned about what pirates were really like. Create a Frequently Asked Questions (FAQ) list with answers to inform people and dispel some of the most common myths about pirates.

_____
_____
_____
_____
_____
_____
_____
_____
_____
_____
_____
_____
_____
_____
_____
_____
_____
_____
_____
_____
_____
_____
_____
_____

Name: _____ **Date:** _____

Directions: Reread "A Sea Shanty." Think about another profession that could inspire folk songs with tales of adventure. Write a poem or song that describes one such adventure.

_____
_____
_____
_____
_____
_____
_____
_____
_____
_____
_____
_____
_____
_____
_____
_____
_____
_____
_____

Directions: Read the text, and answer the questions.

As You Read

Underline information that is new or interesting. Put a star next to information you already knew.

From Wolves to Dogs

Did you know that dogs are direct descendants of wolves? Scientists aren't quite sure whether dogs came from gray wolves or from a type of wolf that has long been extinct. However, most archaeological evidence points to humans domesticating dogs anywhere from 15,000 to 40,000 years ago. During this time, humans had not yet become farmers and were still hunter-gatherers. In fact, humans domesticated dogs long before any cattle, chickens, or other farm animals. In other words, dogs weren't just our ancestors' best friends, they were also their first friends!

Being descendants, however, doesn't mean that dogs and wolves are the same. For instance, you can't really tame a wild wolf. A wolf raised by humans will not replicate dog behavior. And leaving a dog to fend for itself in the woods won't turn it into a wolf. This is because the two subspecies have changed too much over thousands of years.

Today, dogs now come in a large variety of shapes and sizes. They can be bred for hunting, guarding, herding, and more. But despite their differences today, they came from the same place!

1. Which of these is an adjective?

- (A) hunting
- (B) wolf
- (C) really
- (D) extinct

2. Which word is an antonym for *descendants*?

- (A) children
- (B) ancestors
- (C) inheritors
- (D) families

3. Which animal was domesticated first?

- (A) dogs
- (B) chickens
- (C) cows
- (D) pigs

4. What does the prefix *sub–* mean in the word *subspecies*?

- (A) opposite
- (B) under
- (C) more
- (D) not

5. What is a major difference between dogs and wolves?

- (A) Dogs are older than wolves.
- (B) Dogs are larger than wolves.
- (C) Dogs are domesticated, while wolves are not.
- (D) Wolves are domesticated, while dogs are not.

6. What does archaeological evidence tell us about dogs?

- (A) Dogs are descended from gray wolves.
- (B) Dogs are descended from extinct wolves.
- (C) Dogs were domesticated 15,000 to 40,000 years ago.
- (D) Dogs were our ancestors' best friends.

Directions: Read the text, and answer the questions.

As You Read

Underline information that is new or interesting. Put a star next to information you already knew.

How Wolves Became Dogs

Dogs were largely domesticated during the last ice age, which started 33,000 years ago and ended around 14,500 years ago. There are a few theories as to how dogs were domesticated. Some scientists believe that wolves followed humans around and ate their scraps. It is also thought that wolves scavenged leftovers from humans and ate meat that humans discarded. Another theory is that humans domesticated these wolves, either accidentally or on purpose, by feeding them when they came close. These wolves slowly began to trust humans. Eventually, they were helping humans hunt for food.

From there, humans started breeding dogs for specific functions. Collies and shepherds were bred for herding livestock. Pointers and hounds were bred for hunting. Newfoundland dogs were bred for helping with fishing nets. And terriers were bred for catching rats!

Today, dogs come in many different sizes, shapes, colors, and markings. There are hundreds of breeds as well as mutts, or mixed breeds. Many breeds still aid humans, though most dogs are bred simply for their companionship.

1. What can you infer about why wolves became domesticated?

- **A** No one knows the reason for sure.
- **B** Humans were feeding wolves on purpose.
- **C** It happened accidentally.
- **D** Wolves wanted humans to be their companions.

2. What is the meaning of the word *scavenged*?

- **A** hunted an animal
- **B** threw away
- **C** searched through discards
- **D** produced something new

3. The adjective *specific* describes which word?

- **A** started
- **B** we
- **C** breeding
- **D** functions

4. What is the tone of this text?

- **A** informative
- **C** humorous
- **B** persuasive
- **D** inspirational

5. True or false? Every dog is a member of a specific breed.

- **A** true
- **B** false

6. Which is the best summary of this text?

- **A** Wolves were domesticated during the last ice age.
- **B** Humans domesticated dogs because they help us in different ways.
- **C** Today, dogs come in a wide variety of breeds.
- **D** Wolves slowly began to trust humans.

Directions: Read the text, and answer the questions.

As You Read
Underline information that is new or interesting. Put a star next to information you already knew.

How Dogs and Wolves Are Different

If you could stand a wolf next to a dog, you would notice many differences. A wolf's eyes, for instance, are yellow or amber, while a dog's eye color can range from blue to brown. A wolf's head is larger in comparison to its body size than a dog's. A wolf's chest and hips are narrower than a dog's to help with hunting and running through woodlands. Wolves have straight tails, and their giant paws have two extra-large front toes.

One of the main differences between the two animals is that wolves are true pack animals, but dogs are not. In other words, a dog does not consider its owner to be the alpha of the pack. Instead, a dog sees that person more like a family member. A group of dogs that are suddenly let loose from their homes will not form a wolf-like pack. This is because they have been domesticated and no longer have the natural instincts that wolves do. Dogs can show glimpses of these instincts, especially if they are playing with other dogs, but their behavior is not fully comparable to wolf behavior.

1. Which of these are comparative adjectives?

(A) *many* and *any*

(B) *giant* and *raised*

(C) *larger* and *narrower*

(D) *suddenly* and *always*

2. What does the word *alpha* likely mean in this text?

(A) oldest   (C) friend

(B) brother   (D) leader

3. Which of these statements would the author likely agree with?

(A) Wolves are braver than dogs.

(B) Dogs and wolves have nothing in common.

(C) Families and packs have significant differences.

(D) Wolves can learn to be like dogs.

4. Would you rather be a dog or a wolf? Reference details from the text to support your opinion.

_____

_____

_____

_____

5. What is the main idea of this text? Use evidence from the text to support your answer.

_____

_____

_____

Name: _____   Date: _____

The Ties That Bind Dogs and Wolves

Even if you don't have a pet dog, you probably know that they often love to roll around in foul-smelling stuff. This could be mud, a dead animal, poop, garbage, or even places where these things used to be but aren't anymore. This "upside-down dance" includes dogs rubbing their necks, faces, sides, and backs, for a while...unless they're interrupted by their owners. But what meaning or purpose fuels this unusual behavior?

Researchers believe this behavior is a reminder that dogs came from wild wolves. Wolves roll in stinky stuff to communicate to their pack back at home that they have found a potential food source. Imagine that a lone wolf finds a deer carcass, and she rolls around in it, bathing herself in its scent. Then, she goes back to her pack, who instantly recognize the scent. They then know to follow the stinky wolf to their next meal. This behavior is just one example of dog behavior being similar to wolves.

A dog (top) and a wolf (bottom) roll on their backs.

Another similarity between dogs and wolves is how they communicate vocally through barking, growling, whining, yelping, whimpering, and howling. Dogs make these noises for lots of reasons, and some dogs make them more than others. A dog will bark when it is hungry, tired, thirsty, happy, angry, uncomfortable, excited, and more. Overall, dogs bark a lot more than wolves do. Wolves reserve barking for special circumstances, such as to express fear or alarm. For example, a mother wolf who sees a pup near a dangerous riverbank might bark to get their attention.

So many of a dog's behaviors have their roots in wolf behaviors. Does your dog shake and tear apart their squeaky toys? Think about what a wolf might do when it catches wild fowl—ouch! Does your dog love to jump up and down onto you? Consider that wolf pups jump to lick the corner of adult wolves' mouths, triggering the adults to regurgitate food for the pups to eat. Does your dog love to chase cars, mail carriers, squirrels, or rabbits? Your dog is responding to their ancient need to hunt, even if they don't plan on actually hurting anything or anyone. When you consider these deeply rooted behaviors, you can say that your dog is indeed a wild wolf!

Directions: Read "The Ties That Bind Dogs and Wolves." Then, answer the questions.

1. Which of these statements would the author most likely agree with?

   (A) Dog behavior is totally different from wolf behavior.

   (B) Dogs are quieter and calmer than wolves.

   (C) Dogs have many behaviors that have roots in wolf behaviors.

   (D) Dogs and wolves would get along well.

2. Which of the following words is an adverb?

   (A) similarity

   (B) vocally

   (C) communicate

   (D) another

3. What is the meaning of *reserve* in this sentence? *Wolves reserve barking for special circumstances, such as to express fear or alarm.*

   (A) keep for later

   (B) use frequently

   (C) avoid

   (D) repeat

4. What is a reasonable purpose for reading this text?

   (A) to learn how to travel with a dog

   (B) to learn about how dog behavior relates to wolves

   (C) to learn about people's opinions on wolves

   (D) to enjoy a humorous story

5. What is *wild wolf* an example of?

   (A) alliteration

   (B) simile

   (C) metaphor

   (D) satire

6. Compare and contrast wolves and dogs. Record at least two similarities and two differences.

Wolves   **Dogs**

Name: _____ **Date:** _____

Directions: Reread "The Ties That Bind Dogs and Wolves." Then, respond to the prompt.

> Imagine you are a dog. Write a letter to your owner. Explain all the weird things that dogs do and why they do them, from a dog's perspective. Be sure to consider the ways in which dogs are similar to wolves.

_____

_____

_____

_____

_____

_____

_____

_____

_____

_____

_____

_____

_____

_____

_____

_____

_____

_____

_____

_____

_____

_____

_____

_____

Name: _____ **Date:** _____

Directions: Read the text, and answer the questions.

As You Read

Write a ∞ wherever you make connections. Describe your connections in the margins.

Rooster the Dog

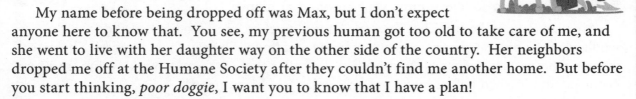

My name is Rooster, but don't get confused because I am actually a dog. The really nice woman at the Humane Society gave me that name when I was dropped off here a few days ago. My fur is sort of orange, my legs are short and squat, and I have a tuft of hair at the top of my head, so all those features reminded her of a rooster. So, I'm perfectly fine with the name and will respond to it moving forward.

My name before being dropped off was Max, but I don't expect anyone here to know that. You see, my previous human got too old to take care of me, and she went to live with her daughter way on the other side of the country. Her neighbors dropped me off at the Humane Society after they couldn't find me another home. But before you start thinking, *poor doggie*, I want you to know that I have a plan!

1. How does Rooster react to his new name?

- (A) He hates it.
- (B) He is confused by it.
- (C) He doesn't mind it.
- (D) He doesn't know it.

2. What kind of sentence is this? *My name before being dropped off was Max, but I don't expect anyone here to know that.*

- (A) simple
- (B) compound
- (C) complex
- (D) compound-complex

3. What is the setting for this text?

- (A) an animal shelter
- (B) the street
- (C) Rooster's house
- (D) a school

4. Which of these events happens last?

- (A) Rooster is given his new name.
- (B) Rooster's owner goes to live with her daughter.
- (C) Rooster is named Max.
- (D) Rooster develops a plan.

5. What sentence from the text is the best evidence that Rooster has a resilient attitude?

- (A) My name is Rooster, but don't get confused because I am actually a dog.
- (B) You see, my previous human got too old to take care of me, and she went to live with her daughter way on the other side of the country.
- (C) My fur is sort of orange, my legs are short and squat, and I have a tuft of hair at the top of my head, so all those features reminded her of a rooster.
- (D) But before you start thinking, *poor doggie*, I want you to know that I have a plan.

Name: _____ Date: _____

Directions: Read the text, and answer the questions.

As You Read

Write a ∞ wherever you make connections. Describe your connections in the margins.

Rooster's Master Plan

The Humane Society is a place where pets who have lost their homes for one reason or another can find new families. There are about 25 of us in the building right now, and each of us have our own small room. Every room is complete with chew toys, a food and water bowl, and warm, cuddly blankets. People come to visit us, and if they find one of us that they really like, they go through an official process called *adoption*. Everyone here refers to it as finding your new forever home.

My plan is to make sure that I am the cutest, quietest, most well-behaved dog in the whole place. This way, I can go to a new home and hopefully stay there forever! The nice woman who named me has given me a bow-tie collar that makes me look dashing, and I was groomed and washed before being put on display for the humans.

But no matter how amazing I look, I seem to be having the worst luck because no one wants to take me home!

1. What is the best summary of Rooster's plan?
   - Ⓐ to get people's attention by barking loudly
   - Ⓑ to show off all his special tricks
   - Ⓒ to be quiet and cute
   - Ⓓ to hide from visitors

2. What type of sentence is this? *But no matter how amazing I look, I seem to be having the worst luck.*
   - Ⓐ simple
   - Ⓑ compound
   - Ⓒ complex
   - Ⓓ compound-complex

3. Which word best describes the feeling Rooster has at the end of this passage?
   - Ⓐ guilty
   - Ⓑ excited
   - Ⓒ proud
   - Ⓓ worried

4. Which word from the text can be both a noun and a verb?
   - Ⓐ place
   - Ⓑ lost
   - Ⓒ get
   - Ⓓ sure

5. What is a good synonym for *dashing* in this phrase? *The nice woman who named me has given me a bow-tie collar that makes me look dashing…*
   - Ⓐ broken
   - Ⓑ handsome
   - Ⓒ silly
   - Ⓓ terrible

Directions: Read the text, and answer the questions.

As You Read

Write a ∞ wherever you make connections. Describe your connections in the margins.

Ol' Man's Advice

No one is picking me, even though I have been giving each human the saddest and cutest expression I can muster. I snuggle in their laps, and I give them a tentative lick or two on their hands to be polite. I make sure to never lick them on their faces, even though I'd really like to!

One day, as I'm working on a new approach and trying out my happy and goofy face, the dog across from me barks to get my attention. It's Ol' Man, the white-muzzled, stringy-haired mutt who has been here longer than any of the other dogs.

"You know that you're going about this the wrong way, right?" Ol' Man says to me.

"No, I don't know that, actually!" I respond, annoyed that Ol' Man is butting in and doubtful that he has any helpful advice. "Isn't it true that the cutest and most fun dogs are the ones basically guaranteed to get forever homes?"

Ol' Man widens his eyes at me, and I start to feel curious, especially since my plan isn't… well…going according to plan.

Ol' Man says, "Humans may pick us, but don't forget that we can also pick the humans."

"That makes about as much sense as taking a bath before going for a roll in the mud," I say.

---

1. What is a likely reason that Ol' Man would want to give Rooster advice?

   Ⓐ They are best friends.

   Ⓑ He is trying to trick Rooster.

   Ⓒ Rooster asked him.

   Ⓓ He wants to share his wisdom.

2. Which is closest to the meaning of *going about this*?

   Ⓐ handling this

   Ⓑ learning this

   Ⓒ watching this

   Ⓓ leaving this

3. What is the best evidence that Rooster was approaching people cautiously?

   Ⓐ "You know that you're going about this the wrong way, right?" Ol' Man says to me.

   Ⓑ It's Ol' Man, the white-muzzled, stringy-haired mutt who has been here longer than any of the other dogs.

   Ⓒ Ol' Man widens his eyes at me, and I start to feel curious, especially since my plan isn't…well…going according to plan.

   Ⓓ I snuggle in their laps, and I give them a tentative lick or two on their hands to be polite. I make sure to never lick them on their faces, even though I'd really like to!

4. What are some differences between Ol' Man and Rooster?

   _____

   _____

Name: _____   Date: _____

As You Read

Write a ∞ wherever you make connections. Describe your connections in the margins.

A Forever Home Found

Ol' Man settles onto his blanket and barks to clear his throat. "I've been in many homes over the years, and the one thing I've learned is that not every forever home is meant to be forever," he says. "Some humans are forgetful and leave you out in the backyard all night. Some humans are not forgetful, but they leave you out in the backyard all night anyway. I guess what I'm trying to say is that you can study humans and know which one will be right for you."

I twitch my tail back and forth as I think about this, and then I ask him, "How do you learn how to do that?"

"First, a good forever-home human won't try to hug you with all their might," Ol' Man says, "because they can feel, or know from previous experience, that we really don't like being squeezed too tight. Also, humans who throw toys at us have obviously never been around dogs before, so they face a steep learning curve. Unless you're a very patient pup, that's a risky situation. So, kid, next time a visitor comes around, notice how they talk to the nice people who work here. Are they gruff or dismissive, or do they fail to hold the door open for someone? Little things like that can say a lot about a person, and you have to watch the parents carefully. If they roll their eyes while watching their kids play with you, they may not really want a dog at all."

Ol' Man has a lot more good advice, but I can't help being bothered by the fact that he is here and not at someone's home. So, I ask him about that.

"Well, regardless of the advice I just gave, the reality is older dogs are often looked over."

Ol' Man assures me he's fine with that, but I see how sad he looks when he's done talking.

A few days later, a human and her child come to visit the Humane Society. Both of them are very nice to the workers, which is my first good sign. Then, the child goes straight to Ol' Man's window, waving at him, and when I get a glimpse of the mother, I can see real kindness in her eyes. The mother steers her child toward me, but I crawl under my blankets and refuse to come out until they go back toward Ol' Man. I know these humans will provide the perfect forever home for him, and I can't get in the way of that. When they go inside his room, his tail just wags and wags, and he's running around the room like a little puppy again.

I'll miss the old guy, but with his helpful advice, I'm sure to find my human soon!

© Shell Education

Directions: Read "A Forever Home Found." Then, answer the questions.

1. Why won't a good human hug a dog tightly at the shelter?

   (A) They want to avoid germs.
   (B) They know dogs don't like it.
   (C) They don't think of it.
   (D) They prefer to play.

2. What is the meaning of the phrase *a steep learning curve*?

   (A) a lot to learn
   (B) a little to learn
   (C) a lot of fun
   (D) a steep hill

3. Which action is a good example of sacrifice?

   (A) Ol' Man shares his advice.
   (B) The mother steers her child toward Rooster.
   (C) Some humans leave dogs out in the backyard all night.
   (D) Rooster hides under the blankets.

4. Which is a good summary of Ol' Man's advice?

   (A) Look for adults with no children.
   (B) Look for humans who have the most children.
   (C) Look for humans who treat each other kindly.
   (D) Look for the calmest humans.

5. What best describes Ol' Man's attitude toward being in the shelter?

   (A) He hates it.
   (B) He loves it.
   (C) He accepts it.
   (D) He is determined to leave.

6. Which is the best antonym for the word *gruff*?

   (A) polite
   (B) blunt
   (C) nasty
   (D) harsh

7. Write behaviors that indicate whether a human is good or bad, according to the story.

Signs of a Good Human	Signs of a Bad Human

Directions: Reread "A Forever Home Found." Then, respond to the prompt.

Write your own version of what happens next to Rooster or to Ol' Man. Start at the line given here.

You never really know what will happen next, though. _____

_____

_____

_____

_____

_____

_____

_____

_____

_____

_____

_____

_____

_____

_____

_____

_____

_____

_____

_____

_____

I Am Not a Dog

One night, while sitting on my human's lap,
something woke me from my nap.
A howling noise from the television
helped me come to a decision.
On the TV was a nature show.
And what I saw led me to know
that I am NOT a dog!
I am...
A WOLF!

Before you scoff and call me a goof,
let me present you with the proof!
Wolves live in packs. That's just like me!
Mine lives in my house and is my family.
Wolves hunt for food. I do the same!
Today, I found stale popcorn behind a picture frame!
Just like a wolf, my fur is thick and fluffy.
Though my groomer trims me as soon as I get scruffy.
That fur protects wolves from the bitter cold.
So does mine...or so I'm told.
Because you know what protects me even better?
My very special doggie sweater!

Yes, you may think I'm an adorable pup,
but now you know what's really up.
I heard all the arguments,
and I know how it seems,
but I am a fearsome wolf in my heart...
and also in my dreams.

Name: _____ Date: _____

Directions: Read "I Am Not a Dog." Then, answer the questions.

1. Which of these words has a positive connotation?
   - (A) scoff
   - (B) bitter
   - (C) fearsome
   - (D) adorable

2. What is the meaning of the idiom *what's really up*?
   - (A) what's new
   - (B) what's happening
   - (C) what's different
   - (D) what's coming

3. What mood is the narrator expressing?
   - (A) confusion
   - (B) anger
   - (C) contentment
   - (D) excitement

4. Why are the words *A WOLF* and *NOT* capitalized?
   - (A) for humor
   - (B) to indicate sarcasm
   - (C) for emphasis
   - (D) to indicate a direct quote

5. Which line best supports the idea that the dog's true nature may not be obvious?
   - (A) Wolves live in packs. That's just like me!
   - (B) Today, I found stale popcorn behind a picture frame!
   - (C) ...and I know how it seems, but I am a fearsome wolf in my heart...
   - (D) A howling noise from the television helped me come to a decision.

6. What is the tone of the poem?
   - (A) aggressive
   - (C) sentimental
   - (B) incredulous
   - (D) humorous

7. What do you imagine this dog's personality is like? Why?

   _____
   _____
   _____
   _____
   _____
   _____

Directions: Closely read these text excerpts. Then, study the poem on page 113. Write words describing the relationship between dogs and people in each text.

Close-Reading Texts

From Wolves to Dogs	A Forever Home Found
Did you know that dogs are direct descendants of wolves? Scientists aren't quite sure whether dogs came from gray wolves or from a type of wolf that has long been extinct. However, most archaeological evidence points to humans domesticating dogs anywhere from 15,000 to 40,000 years ago. During this time, humans had not yet become farmers and were still hunter-gatherers. In fact, humans domesticated dogs long before any cattle, chickens, or other farm animals. In other words, dogs weren't just our ancestors' best friends, they were also their first friends!	"First, a good forever-home human won't try to hug you with all their might," Ol' Man says, "because they can feel, or know from previous experience, that we really don't like being squeezed too tight. Also, humans who throw toys at us have obviously never been around dogs before, so they face a steep learning curve. Unless you're a very patient pup, that's a risky situation. So, kid, next time a visitor comes around, notice how they talk to the nice people who work here. Are they gruff or dismissive, or do they fail to hold the door open for someone? Little things like that can say a lot about a person, and you have to watch the parents carefully. If they roll their eyes while watching their kids play with you, they may not really want a dog at all."

Text	Positive Relationship	Negative Relationship
From Wolves to Dogs		
A Forever Home Found		
I Am Not a Dog		

Name: _____ **Date:** _____

Directions: Closely read these excerpts. Then, compare and contrast wolves and dogs. Record the similarities and differences in the chart, and answer the question.

Close-Reading Texts

How Dogs and Wolves Are Different	I Am Not a Dog
A wolf's eyes, for instance, are yellow or amber, while a dog's eye color can range from blue to brown. A wolf's head is larger in comparison to its body size than a dog's. A wolf's chest and hips are narrower than a dog's to help with hunting and running through woodlands. Wolves have straight tails, and their giant paws have two extra-large front toes. One of the main differences between the two animals is that wolves are true pack animals, but dogs are not. In other words, a dog does not consider its owner to be the alpha of the pack. Instead, a dog sees that person more like a family member. A group of dogs that are suddenly let loose from their homes will not form a wolf-like pack. This is because they have been domesticated and no longer have the natural instincts that wolves do. Dogs can show glimpses of these instincts, especially if they are playing with other dogs, but their behavior is not fully comparable to wolf behavior.	Wolves live in packs. That's just like me! Mine lives in my house and is my family. Wolves hunt for food. I do the same! Today, I found stale popcorn behind a picture frame! Just like a wolf, my fur is thick and fluffy. Though my groomer trims me as soon as I get scruffy. That fur protects wolves from the bitter cold. So does mine…or so I'm told. Because you know what protects me even better? My very special doggie sweater!

	Similarities	Differences
How Dogs and Wolves Are Different		
I Am Not a Dog		

Which text describes wolves as more similar to dogs? Cite evidence to support your answer.

_____

_____

_____

Name: _____ **Date:** _____

Directions: Think about the texts from this unit. Then, respond to the prompt.

Consider all you know about Rooster as a character. Would Rooster rather be a wolf or a dog? Explain your reasoning. Use quotations from the texts as evidence to support your argument.

_____
_____
_____
_____
_____
_____
_____
_____
_____
_____
_____
_____
_____
_____
_____
_____
_____
_____
_____
_____
_____
_____
_____
_____
_____
_____

Name: _____ **Date:** _____

Directions: Reread "I Am Not a Dog." Think about how you also see yourself differently than how others see you. Write an "I Am Not _____" poem that explains who you really are. Be sure to include at least one of the following elements of figurative language: rhyming, repetition, imagery, simile, metaphor, or hyperbole.

_____

_____

_____

_____

_____

_____

_____

_____

_____

_____

_____

_____

_____

_____

_____

_____

_____

_____

_____

_____

_____

_____

_____

_____

_____

Directions: Read the text, and answer the questions.

As You Read
Underline words and phrases that explain what went wrong.

Metric Mistake

On December 11, 1998, the National Aeronautics and Space Administration (NASA) successfully launched a space probe. It was called the Mars Climate Orbiter, and it went all the way to Mars to study its orbit. The journey took nine months. Many scientists and engineers eagerly waited as the probe arrived, preparing to orbit Mars. But instead of orbiting the planet, the probe plunged into the Martian atmosphere. The probe was destroyed. Many questions arose. *What happened? How did the probe end up so far off track? And who was to blame for it all?*

After NASA analyzed the data, they found the problem. NASA revealed that the engineers failed to convert some English measurements to metric, which led to the disaster. In other words, the multi-million dollar project failed due to a simple math mistake! This was an embarrassing moment for NASA. It eroded some of its reputation as a world leader in space exploration.

But thankfully, our mistakes don't usually lead to exploding spacecrafts!

1. What was the mission of the Mars space probe?
   - (A) to land on Mars
   - (B) to orbit Mars
   - (C) to measure the distance between Earth and Mars
   - (D) to carry supplies to the space station

2. Who was to blame for the outcome?
   - (A) administrators
   - (B) astronauts
   - (C) computer programmers
   - (D) engineers

3. Which is a good synonym for *plunged* as it is used in the text?
   - (A) arrived
   - (B) soared
   - (C) rushed
   - (D) plummeted

4. What makes the mistake discussed in this passage especially notable?
   - (A) It happened a long time ago.
   - (B) It cost millions of dollars.
   - (C) It was NASA's first mistake.
   - (D) It resulted in the loss of human life.

5. Which is a good antonym for *eroded* as it is used in the second paragraph?
   - (A) strengthened
   - (B) grinded
   - (C) weakened
   - (D) praised

6. Which of these is an independent clause?
   - (A) on December 11, 1998
   - (B) after NASA analyzed the data
   - (C) they found the problem
   - (D) nine months later

Name: _____ Date: _____

Directions: Read the text, and answer the questions.

As You Read
Circle descriptive language in the text.

The Sloppy Scientist

One of the most consequential scientific mistakes happened in 1928. It ended up changing the world! It all started when scientist Alexander Fleming left a mess in his lab before going on a two-week vacation. When he returned, he had a stack of dirty petri dishes to clean. Some of these dishes had been smeared with Staphylococcus. This is a type of bacteria that causes infections. One of these dishes had an unusual mold growing on it, as dishes left in the sink too long tend to have. This mold, however, did something amazing. It killed the bacteria in the dish!

These results were groundbreaking. Fleming had mistakenly discovered something that could kill harmful bacteria. From his messy mistake, penicillin was born. This is a type of antibiotic that can treat infections. Before this discovery, many injuries, ranging from paper cuts to childbirth, could be deadly. Thanks to Fleming and his accidental mess, people today have a treatment for infections.

1. What literary device is used in the title of this passage?
   - (A) onomatopoeia
   - (B) hyperbole
   - (C) alliteration
   - (D) rhyming

2. Based on this text, what is the effect of leaving the mess in the lab?
   - (A) People got more infections.
   - (B) Most infections were no longer deadly.
   - (C) People no longer needed to wash dishes.
   - (D) Alexander Fleming won an award.

3. Which of these words has a positive connotation?
   - (A) sloppy
   - (B) mistake
   - (C) happened
   - (D) important

4. Which of these words is used as an adverb in the text?
   - (A) bad
   - (B) deadly
   - (C) most
   - (D) important

5. What is the subject of this sentence? *This mold, however, did something amazing.*
   - (A) This
   - (B) mold
   - (C) something
   - (D) amazing

6. Which event happened first?
   - (A) We have treatment for infections.
   - (B) Fleming left a mess.
   - (C) Mold grew.
   - (D) Penicillin was born.

Name: _____ **Date:** _____

Directions: Read the text, and answer the questions.

As You Read
Underline the outcome of each mistake.

Hot and Sticky Mistakes

More scientists have made mistakes that have led to inventions. One example includes an engineer who accidentally melted a chocolate bar in his pocket. In 1945, the engineer was working on a radar project and testing a vacuum tube called a *magnetron*. As he stood near it, the waves from the device melted his lunchtime snack. Realizing the mistake, the engineer then tried it out with popcorn kernels and an egg. He realized he could turn this accident around by using the technology, and the microwave was born!

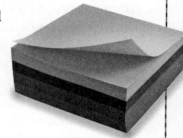

Another example is the invention of sticky notes. The idea behind them started from a mistake by a researcher who failed to invent a really strong glue. The glue he invented was weak, and no one knew what to do with it until a few years later. One of the researcher's colleagues got annoyed when the bookmarks in his church hymnal kept falling out. He remembered the weak glue and tried it out in his book. The rest, as they say, is history!

1. What kind of sentence is this? *Realizing the mistake, the engineer then tried it out with popcorn kernels and an egg.*
   - (A) simple
   - (B) compound
   - (C) complex
   - (D) compound-complex

2. What is an antonym for the word *annoyed*?
   - (A) irritated
   - (B) appeased
   - (C) insulted
   - (D) frustrated

3. Which statement is **not** supported by the text?
   - (A) Accidents can spark great ideas.
   - (B) New inventions can come from unlikely places.
   - (C) Many mistakes have positive outcomes.
   - (D) It's important to be cautious to prevent mistakes when possible.

4. What is the main idea of this passage?

   _____

   _____

   _____

   _____

5. How did luck play a part in the invention of the microwave and sticky notes?

   _____

   _____

   _____

Name: _____   Date: _____

The Key to Mistakes: Learning from Them!

Learning from your mistakes takes some time and effort. The first step is to take responsibility for them. This is what NASA did when they lost their Mars Climate Orbiter. The scientists and engineers admitted that they had made a mistake, and most importantly, they took responsibility for it. They examined what went wrong and found the mistake. The second step to learning from your mistakes involves figuring out a new way forward. In NASA's case, they put procedures in place so a similar mistake wouldn't happen again. NASA could have tried to blame other factors for their mistake, but they chose to take

accountability. The last step in learning from your mistakes involves one of NASA's core values: resilience. Resilience involves recovering or being able to quickly adjust to difficulties. NASA states on their website, "When we put our minds to something—we don't give up. We aren't deterred by obstacles or constraints, and we stay the course to achieve our goals." Resilience can be the key that unlocks a path toward greater success in our lives.

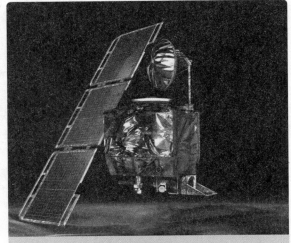

Mars Climate Orbiter

The truth is, everyone hates making mistakes. We're afraid our friends may laugh at us, or we're worried about what our parents might think. We don't want to look silly or stupid or ashamed. However, mistakes are just an unavoidable part of life. And if you really think about it, where would we be without mistakes and failure?

Think about a mistake that you have made at school. Did you mix up a number on a math test and get a bad grade? Did you misinterpret what a certain poem meant in language arts? First, take a breather, and think of how you could have been resilient. Resilience allows people to bounce back after a challenge, and being resilient in the face of failure means not only learning from an experience, but being stronger moving forward.

Reframing your thinking about mistakes can be a useful strategy. Don't feel embarrassed or ashamed of mistakes, and don't think about giving up and saying you're not good at something. Instead, see it as an opportunity to change your thinking. Mistakes can be chances to see what you know, what you thought you knew but didn't, and what you can do moving forward. With this technique, mistakes can jump-start the learning process. Understanding that mistakes create learning opportunities instead of disasters leads people to take more positive risks. And very often, taking risks is what leads to new and wonderful solutions to today's problems!

Directions: Read "The Key to Mistakes: Learning from Them!" Then, answer the questions.

1. What is the author's purpose in writing this passage?

Ⓐ to inform

Ⓑ to persuade

Ⓒ to entertain

Ⓓ to criticize

2. What does the prefix *mis–* mean?

Ⓐ female

Ⓑ behind

Ⓒ wrong

Ⓓ over

3. Which is a good antonym for *resilient*?

Ⓐ defeatist

Ⓑ tough

Ⓒ flexible

Ⓓ robust

4. Is this statement fact or opinion? *They admitted that they had made a mistake.*

Ⓐ fact

Ⓑ opinion

5. Based on the text, which of these statements would the people at NASA disagree with?

Ⓐ Persistence is key to success.

Ⓑ Mistakes are natural.

Ⓒ Ambitious goals are a mistake.

Ⓓ Solutions come from tackling obstacles.

6. Write the pros and cons of making mistakes.

Pros	Cons

Directions: Reread "The Key to Mistakes: Learning from Them." Then, respond to the prompt.

Consider all the pros and cons of making mistakes. Are you comfortable taking risks, or are you more concerned about being embarrassed? Give a few examples of times when you did or did not take a risk that could have led to mistakes or failure. Explain your choice and what happened as a result.

_____
_____
_____
_____
_____
_____
_____
_____
_____
_____
_____
_____
_____
_____
_____
_____
_____
_____
_____
_____
_____
_____
_____
_____
_____
_____

Name: _____   Date: _____

Directions: Read the text, and answer the questions.

As You Read
Write comments and questions you have about the text in the margins.

A New Position

My heart pounds in my chest as I pace the soccer field, nervously hoping that my first time playing this position will go smoothly. I'm used to being a forward with the ball at my feet, ready to score. I've always loved the feeling of beating my defenders and getting a clear kick or pass to a teammate. But I've realized lately that I also love watching our backs and seeing the midfielders defend our goal. So, I've been practicing my defense, and with our normal right defender having to miss our game today, coach is giving me my first chance to play his position!

After playing forward for most of my life, I get the feeling that defending might be easier. There's not as much running in this position, and all I have to do is make sure the ball doesn't end up in our own goal. So really, how hard can it be?

The match starts with the other team, the Pole Cats, kicking off the ball to our midfielder, who clears it to the left wing. One of my teammates gets a clear shot, but the goalie saves it. *Wow*, I think to myself, *it's fun getting to watch the action instead of always being in the middle of things!*

1. What does the word *this* refer to in the phrase *my first time playing this position*?
- (A) left defender
- (B) right defender
- (C) forward
- (D) midfielder

2. What kind of sentence is this? *So, I've been practicing my defense, and with our normal right defender having to miss our game today, coach is giving me my first chance to play his position!*
- (A) simple
- (B) compound
- (C) complex
- (D) compound-complex

3. Which word best describes the narrator's initial attitude toward the difficulty of playing defense?
- (A) insecure
- (B) annoyed
- (C) confident
- (D) vexed

4. Is this statement a fact or an opinion? *Wow, it's fun getting to watch the action instead of always being in the middle of things!*
- (A) fact
- (B) opinion

5. What is a good synonym for the word *position* as it is used in the text?
- (A) figure
- (B) role
- (C) pose
- (D) character

6. What is the setting for this passage?
- (A) a classroom
- (B) a playground
- (C) a soccer field
- (D) a backyard

Name: _____ Date: _____

Directions: Read the text, and answer the questions.

As You Read
Circle and words and phrases that tell you how the narrator is feeling.

Coming My Way

We're 10 minutes into the game, and my first test as a defender comes as one of the Pole Cat strikers streaks down the field right toward me. I run up to face him, and he runs right by me, heading for the goal!

I run to catch up to the ball, and I slide to kick it to my teammate, which sends the striker tumbling down to the ground. It's a foul, and the Pole Cats get a free kick from the sidelines. Now, we have to defend against their shot, and I'm not exactly sure where to stand! I look over, and I can see our coach yelling and pointing to the line of players where he wants me to stand so we can block the shot. I'm standing there, getting ready for the kick, but all I can think about is how the striker got right past me. It was a simple trick because all he did was feint with his head one way and go the other. *Maybe defending isn't going to be as easy as I originally hoped*, I think to myself, sighing.

1. What happens after the narrator trips the opposing player?
   - (A) That player kicks him back.
   - (B) That player keeps running.
   - (C) The opposing team gets a free kick.
   - (D) The opposing team scores.

2. What does the narrator do when he is unsure about where to stand?
   - (A) He picks a random spot.
   - (B) He looks to the coach for guidance.
   - (C) He asks a teammate.
   - (D) He stands as close to the goal as possible.

3. What is a good synonym for *streaks* as it is used in this passage?
   - (A) smears
   - (B) sprints
   - (C) walks
   - (D) dawdles

4. How does the narrator feel about his ability to defend at the end of the passage?
   - (A) apprehensive
   - (B) excited
   - (C) reassured
   - (D) carefree

5. What is closest to the meaning of *feint* in the text?
   - (A) fake
   - (B) follow
   - (C) move
   - (D) fall

6. Based on the text, which of these statements would the narrator most likely agree with?
   - (A) It takes time to learn new skills.
   - (B) The best way to learn new skills is to jump in feet first.
   - (C) New skills require intense studying.
   - (D) Skills are something you are either born with or you're not.

Name: _____ **Date:** _____

Directions: Read the text, and answer the questions.

As You Read

Write comments and questions you have about the text in the margins.

A Series of Unfortunate Mistakes

The next several minutes are hectic because the ball keeps coming my way, and I can't seem to clear it correctly. The first time, I kick it to the middle of the field, and even little kids know that's the worst place to put it. Sure enough, the Pole Cats get the ball and head my way yet again. Our midfielders clear it, and that gives me time to breathe and try to settle down. The next time down the field, the Pole Cats focus on me again, perhaps understanding that I'm starting to panic. All my practicing and training seems to have gone out the window, and now I feel silly for being overconfident before the match. I manage to win the battle for the ball, but feeling totally surrounded, all I can think to do is kick the ball out of bounds. I can sense my teammates looking at me, wondering why I didn't try to cross the ball down the field. I don't know what happened, but I know one way I can make it up to them!

1. Which is a good antonym for the word *surrounded* as it is used in this text?
   - (A) besieged
   - (B) encircled
   - (C) insulated
   - (D) alone

2. Which word best describes how the narrator is feeling in this passage?
   - (A) arrogant
   - (B) on top of things
   - (C) electrified
   - (D) overwhelmed

3. Which of these is a dependent clause?
   - (A) the next several minutes are hectic
   - (B) the next time down the field
   - (C) but I know one way I can make it up to them
   - (D) the Pole Cats get the ball and head my way yet again

4. Which of these statements from the text is the best evidence that the new position is stressful?
   - (A) I don't know what happened, but I know one way I can make it up to them!
   - (B) Our midfielders clear it.
   - (C) ...perhaps understanding that I'm starting to panic.
   - (D) I manage to win the battle for the ball.

5. What do you predict the main character will do to make up for his mistake?

_____

_____

_____

Learning from My Mistakes

There's two minutes until halftime, and I really want to make up for my mistake. Here comes my chance as I win the ball from the Pole Cat striker, and I decide that enough is enough! I run down the field dribbling the ball past defenders (and teammates) with nothing else on my mind except scoring. I keep going until I lose the ball and realize that by leaving my defending position, the Pole Cats now have a better chance at scoring. I run back as fast as I can, but it's too late, and they score!

I put my head in my hands, knowing my mistake might cost us the game. I peek up at our coach, but he's just clapping his hands and saying, "That's okay, get your head back in the game."

I keep thinking he's going to replace me, but then it's half time, thankfully! A few teammates pat me on the back as we head to the locker room, but I am in no mood for being consoled. I just want to get out of the game, so when I see our coach, I ask him to take me out.

Coach takes me aside and asks, "Do you really want me to take you out of the match, or do you want to prove that you can learn from your mistakes? Don't answer that now, but by the end of halftime, tell me what you want to do."

I sit down and drink some water, feeling like I know that my answer is already "take me out right away!" Still, I heed our coach's advice, and I think about everything that went wrong out there. First, I tried clearing the ball to the center of the field, which is a big no-no. Then, I left my position without any back-up plan as I tried to be the hero, which led to the goal. I know better than that; I know my role as a defender doesn't involve as much action as a forward position. But there is something else that's bothering me…I'm panicking, and I know what to do when I feel panicky. My dad taught me to breathe, silence my worries, and let the game come to me. If I can stop trying to be perfect and just do what I can, the action on the field slows down. This way, I don't have to overthink or react too quickly, forcing a bad decision.

At the end of half time, our coach comes up to me as he's finishing a peanut butter and jelly sandwich, and he asks me what I figured out while I was sitting here. I tell him that I make bad decisions when I'm too much in my head and panicking. Then, I tell him that I want to stay on the field—I want to prove to him (and myself) that I won't make the same mistakes again. I just need time to prove it.

135158—180 Days of Reading

Directions: Read "Learning from My Mistakes." Then, answer the questions.

1. What does the narrator try to do to make up for his earlier mistakes?

- Ⓐ double down on defense
- Ⓑ trick the opponents
- Ⓒ score for his team
- Ⓓ block a shot

2. Which of the following is **not** a consequence of the narrator panicking on the field?

- Ⓐ leaving his position
- Ⓑ overanalyzing
- Ⓒ making mistakes
- Ⓓ making good decisions

3. Why does Coach ask the narrator to wait until the end of halftime?

- Ⓐ It's very loud at halftime.
- Ⓑ He wants the narrator to reconsider sitting out.
- Ⓒ Coach thinks it's a good idea for the narrator to sit out.
- Ⓓ The coach is hungry.

4. Which of these words is used as an adjective in the first paragraph?

- Ⓐ mistake
- Ⓑ decide
- Ⓒ keep
- Ⓓ defending

5. Which is a good synonym for *back-up* as it is used in paragraph 5?

- Ⓐ secondary
- Ⓑ reverse
- Ⓒ behind
- Ⓓ past

6. Which event happens first?

- Ⓐ The coach eats a peanut butter and jelly sandwich.
- Ⓑ The Pole Cats score.
- Ⓒ Halftime starts.
- Ⓓ The narrator asks to be taken out of the game.

7. Summarize the main problem in the text, the narrator's reaction, and his solution.

Problem	Narrator's Reaction	Solution

Name: _____ **Date:** _____

Directions: Reread "Learning from My Mistakes." Then, respond to the prompt.

You decide whether the second half went better or worse for the narrator. Then write a diary entry as the narrator. Write in first-person perspective. Describe how the game went and how you felt. What lessons did you learn?

_____

_____

_____

_____

_____

_____

_____

_____

_____

_____

_____

_____

_____

_____

_____

_____

_____

_____

_____

_____

_____

_____

_____

_____

Name: _____ Date: _____

Unit 7
WEEK 3
DAY 1

IN TODAY'S NEWS

Newspaper editors have many important jobs. This includes choosing the stories they're going to run, editing the stories, and coming up with catchy headlines. With so much on their plate, sometimes newspaper editors make mistakes. For example, see the following headlines.

Storewide Sale! 100% Off All Furniture!

Missippi's Literacy Program Shows Improvement

'We Hate Math,' Say 4 In 10— a Majority of Americans

TWINS BORN 10 MONTHS EARLY

Amphibious Baseball Fielder Makes Debut

STUDENTS COOK AND SERVE GRANDPARENTS

Scientists Say **Human Brian Still Evolving**

Safety Meeting Ends in Accident

BREATHING OXYGEN LINKED TO **STAYING ALIVE**

How to Buy a $450,000 Home for Only $700,000!

Think of a Headline 56pt. Bold Headline

NORTHFIELD PLANS TO PLAN STRATEGIC PLAN

© Shell Education

135158—180 Days of Reading

Name: _____   Date: _____

Directions: Read "In Today's News." Then, answer the questions.

1. Which mistake is **not** present in these headlines?

   Ⓐ spelling errors
   Ⓑ miscalculations
   Ⓒ repetition
   Ⓓ vague pronouns

2. Which word would best replace *Amphibious* in the headline *Amphibious Baseball Fielder Makes Debut*?

   Ⓐ ambiguous
   Ⓑ human
   Ⓒ ambidextrous
   Ⓓ ambiance

3. What is the likely explanation for the error in the headline, *Think of a Headline 56 pt. Bold Headline*?

   Ⓐ forgetfulness
   Ⓑ poor grammar
   Ⓒ poor spelling
   Ⓓ computer malfunction

4. What is closest to the meaning of *on their plate* as it is used in this text?

   Ⓐ in their meal
   Ⓑ in their office
   Ⓒ as an option
   Ⓓ as part of their duties

5. How could you change this headline to be clearer? *Students Cook and Serve Grandparents*

   Ⓐ Students Cook and Serve Their Grandparents
   Ⓑ Students Cook and Serve Grandparents Alone
   Ⓒ Students Cook and Serve Meals to Their Grandparents
   Ⓓ Students and Grandparents Cook and Serve

6. Which of these words is a good replacement for *to Plan* in this headline, *Northfield Plans to Plan a Strategic Plan*?

   Ⓐ to create   Ⓒ to return
   Ⓑ to investigate   Ⓓ to intend

7. List four different headlines from page 131. Then, identify the error and explain how you would fix it.

Headline	Error	How to Fix It

Name: _____ **Date:** _____

Directions: Closely read these excerpts. Then, review the headlines on page 131. Explain how each text describes the consequences of a mistake.

Close-Reading Texts

Metric Mistake	Learning from My Mistakes
On December 11, 1998, the National Aeronautics and Space Administration (NASA) successfully launched a space probe. It was called the Mars Climate Orbiter, and it went all the way to Mars to study its orbit. The journey took nine months. Many scientists and engineers eagerly waited as the probe arrived, preparing to orbit Mars. But instead of orbiting the planet, the probe plunged into the Martian atmosphere. The probe was destroyed. Many questions arose. *What happened? How did the probe end up so far off track? And who was to blame for it all?* After NASA analyzed the data, they found the problem. NASA revealed that the engineers failed to convert some English measurements to metric, which led to the disaster. In other words, the multi-million dollar project failed due to a simple math mistake! This was an embarrassing moment for NASA. It eroded some of its reputation as a world leader in space exploration.	There's two minutes until halftime, and I really want to make up for my mistake. Here comes my chance as I win the ball from the Pole Cat striker, and I decide that enough is enough! I run down the field dribbling the ball past defenders (and teammates) with nothing else on my mind except scoring. I keep going until I lose the ball and realize that by leaving my defending position, the Pole Cats now have a better chance at scoring. I run back as fast as I can, but it's too late, and they score!

Metric Mistake	Learning from My Mistakes	In Today's News

Name: _____ **Date:** _____

Directions: Closely read these excerpts. Then, compare and contrast the way NASA and the narrator of the story responded to mistakes they made.

Close-Reading Texts

The Key to Mistakes: Learning from Them!	Learning from My Mistakes
Learning from your mistakes takes some time and effort. The first step is to take responsibility for them. This is what NASA did when they lost their Mars Climate Orbiter. The scientists and engineers admitted that they had made a mistake, and most importantly, they took responsibility for it. They examined what went wrong and found the mistake. The second step to learning from your mistakes involves figuring out a new way forward. In NASA's case, they put procedures in place so a similar mistake wouldn't happen again. NASA could have tried to blame other factors for their mistake, but they chose to take accountability. The last step in learning from your mistakes involves one of NASA's core values: resilience. Resilience involves recovering or being able to quickly adjust to difficulties. NASA states on their website, "When we put our minds to something—we don't give up. We aren't deterred by obstacles or constraints, and we stay the course to achieve our goals." Resilience can be the key that unlocks a path toward greater success in our lives.	Still, I heed our coach's advice, and I think about everything that went wrong out there. First, I tried clearing the ball to the center of the field, which is a big no-no. Then, I left my position without any back-up plan as I tried to be the hero, which led to the goal. I know better than that; I know my role as a defender doesn't involve as much action as a forward position. But there is something else that's bothering me...I'm panicking, and I know what to do when I feel panicky. My dad taught me to breathe, silence my worries, and let the game come to me. If I can stop trying to be perfect and just do what I can, the action on the field slows down. This way, I don't have to overthink or react too quickly, forcing a bad decision.

At the end of half time, our coach comes up to me as he's finishing a peanut butter and jelly sandwich, and he asks me what I figured out while I was sitting here. I tell him that I make bad decisions when I'm too much in my head and panicking. Then, I tell him that I want to stay on the field—I want to prove to him (and myself) that I won't make the same mistakes again. |

NASA   **Narrator**

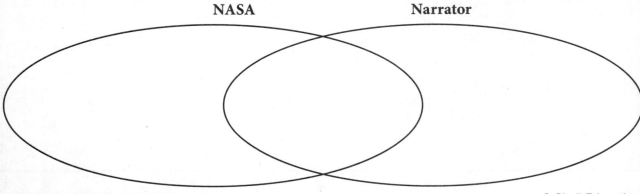

135158—180 Days of Reading   © Shell Education

Name: _____ **Date:** _____

Directions: Think about the texts from this unit. Then, respond to the prompt.

How have you responded in the past when you have made a mistake? What was the outcome? Create two comic strips. The first one should depict a mistake you made and how you handled it. The second one should depict how you would have handled it if you could go back in time and do it perfectly.

Name: _____ Date: _____

Directions: Think about the major events in your life, good and bad. Write catchy headlines to summarize each. Use techniques such as humor and alliteration to catch people's attention.

Name: _____ Date: _____

Directions: Read the text, and answer the questions.

How Clouds Form

The clouds in the sky can capture our imaginations. We may spy a cloud shaped like a wolf howling, while another cloud might make us think of a dinosaur stalking its prey. Sometimes, clouds look wispy and fluffy as they scatter across the sky. But clouds can also grow dark and ominous, serving as a signal of thunderous storms to come. Clouds are always shape-shifting, and they serve many important functions for the planet.

You might be wondering how clouds form in the sky. The whole process starts with bodies of water across the planet. Oceans surround the continents, and rivers crisscross through countries. In time, some of this water evaporates into Earth's atmosphere. The liquid water transforms into water vapor, which is an invisible gas. As water vapor rises in the sky, the surrounding air cools in temperature. Water vapor begins to stick to tiny particles in the air, such as dust. Clouds form when water vapor changes into liquid water droplets, which take shape around the tiny particles. Millions of these water droplets come together to form clouds high up in the sky. Eventually, rain or snow falls from the clouds, and water returns to Earth's surface.

1. Which is a good synonym for the word *spy* as it is used in the first paragraph?

   (A) detective   (C) infiltrator

   (B) find   (D) stalk

2. What is the main idea of the first paragraph?

   (A) Clouds are varied and fascinating.

   (B) Clouds are formed through a process of evaporation.

   (C) Clouds are fun to look at, but not important.

   (D) Clouds always indicate a storm is coming.

3. What kind of connotation does the word *ominous* have?

   (A) positive   (B) negative

4. What does the suffix *–let* mean in the word *droplet*?

   (A) person   (C) full of

   (B) small   (D) without

5. What is the first effect of water vapor rising up in the sky?

   (A) Snow falls from the sky.

   (B) Clouds become wispier.

   (C) Water vapor sticks to tiny particles.

   (D) Oceans surround the continents.

6. What is the meaning of the phrase *capture our imaginations* as it is used in the first sentence?

   (A) distract us

   (B) confuse us

   (C) be interesting to us

   (D) leave nothing to the imagination

Name: _____   Date: _____

Directions: Read the text, and answer the questions.

Thanks to Clouds

Clouds play a big role in shaping Earth's weather and climate in a few ways. First, clouds are crucial in Earth's water cycle because they help produce precipitation, such as rain and snow. Without water, all living things on Earth would eventually die, so clouds can be helpful in returning moisture to Earth. Second, clouds regulate and control global temperatures. Scientists sometimes refer to clouds as an "atmospheric blanket." This is because solar energy from the sun bounces off clouds and returns to space. This reflection of sunlight helps ensure that temperatures on the planet don't rise too high. Clouds can also return heat to the planet. Heat is released from Earth's surface, and clouds sometimes take in this heat. Clouds can return this heat to the planet, which warms up the ground and certain areas of the atmosphere. Ultimately, clouds can have either a cooling or warming effect on the planet. Clouds that are closer to the planet's surface are more likely to help cool temperatures. Clouds that are higher in the sky will probably warm up Earth's surface. Without the help of clouds, Earth's weather and climate would be very different!

1. True or false? Without clouds, life on Earth would end.
   - (A) true
   - (B) false

2. What is the role of clouds as an "atmospheric blanket"?
   - (A) to comfort people
   - (B) to stabilize temperatures
   - (C) to create a view
   - (D) to entertain people

3. What is the meaning of the prefix *atmo–* as in the word *atmosphere*?
   - (A) new
   - (B) placed
   - (C) vapor
   - (D) after

4. Which is the best summary of this passage?
   - (A) Clouds are not just pretty to look at.
   - (B) Clouds keep the Earth from getting too hot.
   - (C) Clouds cool Earth's surface so it doesn't get too hot.
   - (D) Clouds return water to the surface and help regulate temperatures.

5. What part of speech is the word *too* in this sentence? *This reflection of sunlight helps ensure that temperatures on the planet don't rise too high.*
   - (A) noun
   - (B) verb
   - (C) adjective
   - (D) adverb

6. Based on this passage, which word would the author most likely use to describe clouds?
   - (A) vital
   - (B) immobile
   - (C) impractical
   - (D) common

Directions: Read the text, and answer the questions.

As You Read
Circle descriptive language related to clouds.

Cloudy Q&A

Clouds create a white, stark contrast against blue skies. But have you ever wondered why clouds are nearly always a white color? This is because the water droplets that make up a cloud are often squeezed very tightly together. When sunlight travels through a cloud, the water droplets reflect nearly all the light that strikes them. When all the wavelengths of sunlight blend together, a white color is visible to the human eye. Since clouds reflect most of the sunlight that travels through them, humans see clouds as a white color, too.

Clouds may look like light, fluffy cotton in the sky, but did you also know clouds can weigh a lot? From far away, clouds might seem weightless, especially since they float in the sky. However, clouds appear to "float" in the air because they are made of moist air. Moist air has less density, or parts that are close together, compared to dry air. Since clouds are less dense, they can remain in the sky. The weight of different clouds will vary, but an average cumulus cloud can weigh around 1.1 million pounds (498,952 kilograms)!

1. How do clouds "float" in the sky?
   - (A) They are held up by winds.
   - (B) They are exceptionally light.
   - (C) They are less dense than dry air.
   - (D) Water always floats.

2. Why do clouds usually look white to us?
   - (A) They are frozen water, which looks white.
   - (B) Most of the sunlight reflects off the water droplets.
   - (C) They are too far away to see the actual color.
   - (D) Most of the sunlight is absorbed by the water droplets.

3. True or false? Clouds can weigh thousands or even millions of pounds.
   - (A) true
   - (B) false

4. Which word is modified by *weightless* in this sentence? *From far away, clouds might seem weightless, especially since they float in the sky.*
   - (A) seem
   - (B) far
   - (C) clouds
   - (D) float

5. What is the main idea of the second paragraph?

   _____

   _____

6. Does it make you nervous to think about lots of water floating over your head? Why or why not?

   _____

   _____

Name: _____ Date: _____

As You Read
Circle each category and type of cloud listed.

Cloud Atlas

Because clouds come in many shapes and sizes, scientists created a classification system. This "cloud atlas" can help people pinpoint what kind of cloud they're looking at. It can also help them forecast upcoming weather. Most clouds can be divided into three major categories: high clouds, mid-level clouds, and low clouds. Each category has different characteristics.

The first category is high clouds. These clouds are about 10,000 to 60,000 feet (3,048 to 18,288 meters) high. Cirrus, cirrostratus, and cirrocumulus are all high clouds. High clouds are usually white in color. Ice crystals usually form cirrus clouds, which are wispy, feathery clouds. Cirrostratus clouds are often spotted in the winter and cover the sky in a thin, whitish cloak. These clouds could signal that rain or snow is coming within a day! Cirrocumulus clouds often group together to look like a white, crinkled sheet stretched across the sky.

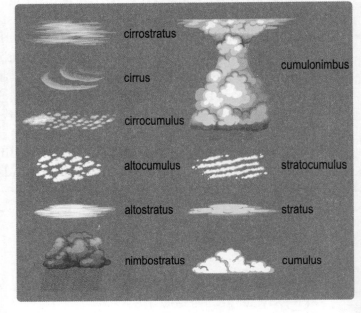

The second category is mid-level clouds. Mid-level clouds usually drift between 6,000 to 25,000 feet (1,829 to 7,620 meters) high. Altocumulus, altostratus, and nimbostratus are all mid-level clouds. They are often grey in color. Also, they seem to create layers of clouds in the sky. Altocumulus clouds look like patchy rows of grey and white. Altostratus clouds create a grey, all-encompassing blanket over the sky. These clouds might signal that a storm or lots of rain lies ahead! Nimbostratus clouds are dense and dark, and they completely mask the sun. Rain or snow often falls from nimbostratus clouds.

The last category is low clouds. Low clouds hang out around 6,500 feet (1,981 meters) or lower. There are four different types. The two most common are cumulus and stratus clouds. Cumulus clouds are big, fluffy white clouds that can morph into many shapes. Stratus clouds thinly stretch over the sky and can create a sense of grey gloom. Two other types of low clouds are cumulonimbus and stratocumulus. Cumulonimbus clouds emerge on hot days and can look like dramatic mountains in the sky. Watch out for these clouds because they usually indicate a big storm or tornado is on the way! Stratocumulus clouds are often compared to the look of a honeycomb, and they are spotty and uneven grey or white clouds.

These are just 10 of the major cloud formations, but there are many more! See how many of them you can spy the next time you look up at the sky.

Directions: Read "Cloud Atlas." Then, answer the questions.

1. What are clouds categorized by in the three major categories?

   Ⓐ size

   Ⓑ height

   Ⓒ storm type

   Ⓓ density

2. Which is a good synonym for the word *wispy* as it is used in the passage?

   Ⓐ delicate

   Ⓑ heavy

   Ⓒ substantial

   Ⓓ crinkly

3. Which type of clouds often indicate a tornado is coming?

   Ⓐ cirrus

   Ⓑ cirrocumulus

   Ⓒ cumulonimbus

   Ⓓ stratus

4. What kind of sentence is this? *Stratocumulus clouds are often compared to the look of a honeycomb, and they are spotty and uneven grey or white clouds.*

   Ⓐ simple

   Ⓑ compound

   Ⓒ complex

   Ⓓ compound-complex

5. Record the different types of clouds in each category.

High	Mid-Level	Low

Name: _____   Date: _____

Directions: Reread "Cloud Atlas." Then, respond to the prompt.

Create a pictorial cloud atlas using the descriptions of different cloud types in the text. For each type, include a picture, a brief description, and where it is usually located. Clouds to include: cirrus, cirrocumulus, altostratus, nimbostratus, cumulus, and cumulonimbus.

Directions: Read the text, and answer the questions.

As You Read
Underline words and phrases that show you how Donatello is feeling.

Donatello Hears from Mother Nature

It took Donatello 18 years to become the Cloud Conjurer. This was the official title given to the sculptor of Earth's clouds. Every day, Donatello sat in his tiny studio and sculpted the clouds that people would see in sky. He was proud of everything he had accomplished in his (relatively) young lifetime.

But lately, Donatello had been struggling to create something *new*. He didn't think anyone else had noticed his lack of cloud variety, but apparently, Mother Nature had. Last week, Mother Nature sent him a pigeon with a missive tied to its foot.

"My dear," Mother Nature wrote, "You know I am largely a fan of those cumulus clouds you love to shape and mold. However, I think the humans are growing a bit bored with those fluffy cotton balls. I want you to dig a bit deeper into your imagination. Please come up with a new and creative cloud design, and remember that the sky is your canvas!"

A new kind of cloud required many different ingredients. Donatello had no clue where to begin, especially now that he knew Mother Nature was watching!

1. What is a *missive*?
   - (A) a pet
   - (B) a message
   - (C) a book
   - (D) a bill

2. What is the best alternative job title for Donatello?
   - (A) Cloud Seller
   - (B) Cloud Destroyer
   - (C) Cloud Painter
   - (D) Cloud Creator

3. What does the word *this* refer to in this sentence? *This was the official title given to the sculptor of Earth's clouds.*
   - (A) Donatello
   - (B) Cloud Conjurer
   - (C) title
   - (D) clouds

4. Which word best describes how Donatello is feeling after reading the missive?
   - (A) queasy
   - (B) confident
   - (C) hurt
   - (D) overwhelmed

5. What is the setting of this story?
   - (A) on a cloud
   - (B) in an office building
   - (C) in a sculptor's studio
   - (D) in a school

6. Which is the best antonym for *variety* as it is used in the text?
   - (A) monotony
   - (B) diversity
   - (C) assortment
   - (D) novelty

Name: _____ **Date:** _____

Directions: Read the text, and answer the questions.

As You Read

Underline what Donatello likes to do, and circle what he didn't like.

Donatello Stares at the Sky

Donatello was the kind of sculptor who liked to putter around his studio. On a regular work week, he usually spent at least two days just staring at the ceiling. Donatello deeply believed that his daydreaming helped him come up with more creative ideas. The sculptor's best ideas usually dropped into his brain without warning.

For instance, Donatello's idea for lenticular clouds came on a random Tuesday as he was bouncing a rubber ball off his studio wall. The image for round discs of clouds in the sky just leapt into his brain. That afternoon, he hurried around his studio, molding and shaping this new cloud. He needed specific environmental conditions to make lenticular clouds. This new kind of cloud could only form when air gusted across mountains.

When he finally showed off the lenticular cloud design in the skies, Donatello listened closely to the humans' critiques.

"Those look like pancakes," said one human who saw the new clouds. Another human claimed they looked like spaceship saucers. Donatello grinned in pride. He loved it when the humans saw different shapes in his clouds.

But now, he was completely and utterly stuck, unable to think of a new cloud idea.

1. What is Donatello doing when he is not being productive?

   (A) daydreaming
   (B) waiting for inspiration
   (C) bouncing balls
   (D) all of the above

2. Which word best describes Donatello's preferred work style?

   (A) intense   (C) frantic
   (B) consistent   (D) relaxed

3. Where does Donatello usually get feedback on his designs?

   (A) from Mother Nature
   (B) from listening to humans
   (C) from other cloud designers
   (D) only from himself

4. What kind of connotation does the word *stuck* have in this text?

   (A) positive
   (B) negative
   (C) neutral

5. What kind of clause is this? *When he finally showed off the lenticular cloud design in the skies*

   (A) dependent
   (B) independent

6. What does the word *putter* suggest about Donatello?

   (A) He prefers to sit in a corner.
   (B) He runs quickly.
   (C) He concentrates intently.
   (D) He walks around to think.

Directions: Read the text, and answer the questions.

As You Read
Underline Donatello's excuses.

Donatello Faces His Fear

Donatello did not like to ask for help, but when he did, he turned to Frida, who was in charge of sculpting flowers for Mother Nature. He went to Frida's sunny apartment that afternoon, and over two cups of coffee, Frida asked Donatello what was holding his creativity back.

Donatello gave his usual list of excuses. He talked about how insistent Mother Nature was and how he could not be expected to meet tight deadlines. He complained about how there was just not enough time for him to be creative. Frida listened, but Donatello saw from her expression that she was unimpressed with this list of excuses. Finally, Frida held up a hand to stop him.

"Tell me, Donatello, what are you most fearful of?" Frida asked him.

Donatello's greatest strength was that he could hear a question and answer it with his heart, rather than his brain. He took a moment to think deeply on his feelings, and he said the first thing that blossomed to the surface: "I am scared to fail."

Frida nodded her head, gently placing her hand on his arm. "But Donatello, it is okay to fail. And, to be creative, you may need to fail a time or two."

1. What can you infer about Donatello because he does not like to ask for help?
   - (A) He is lonely.
   - (B) He is self-reliant.
   - (C) He is selfish.
   - (D) He is a poor communicator.

2. What is Donatello's greatest fear?
   - (A) fear itself
   - (B) listening to others
   - (C) failure
   - (D) success

3. Which of these is **not** a conjunction?
   - (A) so
   - (B) but
   - (C) and
   - (D) They are all conjunctions.

4. Which word best describes Frida's response to Donatello's list of excuses?
   - (A) annoyed
   - (B) compassionate
   - (C) amused
   - (D) joyful

5. How does Frida help Donatello?

_____

_____

6. What do you predict Donatello will do next? Why?

_____

_____

Donatello Sculpts a New Cloud

Donatello never liked to fail, but he felt the truth in Frida's words. He knew that every artist failed a few times when they were creating their works of art. Not everything he created would be a resounding success, he realized. And Frida had helped him understand that it was okay to not get everything right on the first try. With this knowledge, Donatello felt the freedom to create again.

On his way back from Frida's apartment, Donatello walked by the ocean. The ocean's waves crashed and rolled backwards and forwards. He looked out at the mesmerizing and shape-shifting ocean. He was reminded of his clouds and how they liked to re-shape and shift into new forms. As Donatello stared out at the waves, the canvas inside his head was quickly covered in imaginative brush strokes. A vision for a new cloud appeared, a cloud that could mirror the waves slapping against the shoreline.

In his studio, Donatello hurried to capture his new idea. He looked through his ingredient list, determining how he could use atmospheric conditions to sculpt his new clouds. He determined that the conditions needed to be unstable. These new clouds needed to occur alongside altocumulus and stratocumulus clouds.

Donatello sculpted and re-sculpted, and he completely lost track of time as he worked. He was so immersed in his work that he barely registered his doorbell ringing. He ran down, opening the door to Mother Nature, who entered his studio with a smile.

"What new clouds have you sculpted for me and Earth, Donatello?" she asked.

Instead of showing her his sculptures, Donatello took Mother Nature to the rooftop of his place, where he had mixed and melded the ingredients he needed. Donatello blew some wind through his fingers, and his new clouds took to the sky in chaotic waves.

Donatello and Mother Nature craned their necks, peering up at the sky, as the new clouds rolled across. Donatello's new clouds formed ripples and waves. While some of the clouds were smooth, others had rough edges. Donatello watched as the skies transformed into a chaotic ocean of clouds.

He looked over at Mother Nature, who clapped her hands in delight.

"I believe the humans will call these 'asperitas clouds,'" she mused, "and they will find them both terrifying and delightful."

Mother Nature smiled at him, and Donatello felt the gratitude in her glance. Mother Nature left him on the roof, and Donatello stared up at his new clouds, his creativity in flight.

Directions: Read "Donatello Sculpts a New Cloud." Then, answer the questions.

1. What inspires Donatello's ides for a new type of cloud?
- (A) Frida's house
- (B) ocean waves
- (C) stratocumulus clouds
- (D) mirrors

2. How does Mother Nature respond to the new clouds?
- (A) with disappointment
- (B) with acceptance
- (C) with pleasure
- (D) with disapproval

3. What is a synonym for *immersed*, as it is used in paragraph 4?
- (A) engrossed
- (B) inside
- (C) dunked
- (D) distracted

4. Which word is **not** used to describe the new clouds?
- (A) chaotic
- (B) terrifying
- (C) delightful
- (D) familiar

5. What kind of environmental conditions does Donatello need for the new clouds?
- (A) stable
- (B) fixed
- (C) erratic
- (D) warm

6. Which two words can be used as synonyms of each other?
- (A) *mixed* and *melded*
- (B) *creativity* and *truth*
- (C) *smooth* and *rough*
- (D) *capture* and *create*

7. Record the words used to describe ocean waves and asperitas clouds.

Ocean Waves	Asperitas Clouds

Name: _____ **Date:** _____

Directions: Reread "Donatello Sculpts a New Cloud." Then, respond to the prompt.

> If you could create a new version of something in nature, what would it be? Draw a new design, and describe what makes it special.

_____

_____

_____

_____

_____

_____

_____

_____

_____

_____

_____

The Cloud
by Sara Teasdale

I am a cloud in the heaven's height,
The stars are lit for my delight,
Tireless and changeful, swift and free,
I cast my shadow on hill and sea—
But why do the pines on the mountain's crest
Call to me always, "Rest, rest?"

I throw my mantle over the moon
And I blind the sun on his throne at noon,
Nothing can tame me, nothing can bind,
I am a child of the heartless wind—
But oh the pines on the mountain's crest
Whispering always, "Rest, rest."

Sara Teasdale was an American poet. She was born on August 8, 1884. During her lifetime, she published seven books of poetry. In 1915, she published *Rivers to the Sea*, which included "The Cloud."

Teasdale's poems often feature short, clear, and heartfelt lyrics. Her writing developed over the years and reflected her shifting perspective on life, love, and death. She often wrote poems in verse forms, such as quatrains or sonnets. Her fourth book, *Love Song*, won the Columbia University Poetry Society Prize. This prize later became the Pulitzer Prize for Poetry.

Teasdale died in 1933. Her last collection of poetry, *Strange Victory*, was published after her death.

Name: _____ Date: _____

Directions: Read "The Cloud." Then, answer the questions.

1. Which rhyme pattern does this poem use?

   (A) ABAB   (C) ABBA
   (B) AABBCC   (D) AABBA

2. Which element of figurative language is used throughout the poem?

   (A) simile
   (B) metaphor
   (C) personification
   (D) hyperbole

3. What do the first two lines of the second stanza mean?

   (A) The cloud is present at night.
   (B) The cloud blocks light from the sun and moon.
   (C) The cloud hides from the sun and moon.
   (D) The cloud is very high in the sky.

4. What perspective is this poem written in?

   (A) first person
   (B) second person
   (C) third person
   (D) first and second person

5. How is the wind described?

   (A) strong
   (B) callous
   (C) fierce
   (D) demonstrative

6. Which element of figurative language is **not** used in this poem?

   (A) alliteration
   (B) rhyme
   (C) repetition
   (D) onomatopoeia

7. Summarize how each stanza describes the cloud and the actions the cloud takes.

	Description	Actions
Stanza 1		
Stanza 2		

Directions: Closely read these paragraphs. Then, review the poem on page 149. Look for physical and emotional descriptions of clouds. Record the information in the chart.

Close-Reading Texts

How Clouds Form	Donatello Sculpts a New Cloud
The clouds in the sky can capture our imaginations. We may spy a cloud shaped like a wolf howling, while another cloud might make us think of a dinosaur stalking its prey. Sometimes, clouds look wispy and fluffy as they scatter across the sky. But clouds can also grow dark and ominous, serving as a signal of thunderous storms to come. Clouds are always shape-shifting, and they serve many important functions for the planet.	On his way back from Frida's apartment, Donatello walked by the ocean. The ocean's waves crashed and rolled backwards and forwards. He looked out at the mesmerizing and shape-shifting ocean. He was reminded of his clouds and how they liked to re-shape and shift into new forms. As Donatello stared out at the waves, the canvas inside his head was quickly covered in imaginative brush strokes. A vision for a new cloud appeared, a cloud that could mirror the waves slapping against the shoreline.

How Clouds Form	Donatello Sculpts a New Cloud	The Cloud

Name: _____ Date: _____

Directions: Closely read these paragraphs. Then, compare and contrast the explanations of how clouds are formed.

Close-Reading Texts

How Clouds Form	Donatello Stares at the Sky
You might be wondering how clouds form in the sky. The whole process starts with bodies of water across the planet. Oceans surround the continents, and rivers crisscross through countries. In time, some of this water evaporates into Earth's atmosphere. The liquid water transforms into water vapor, which is an invisible gas. As water vapor rises in the sky, the surrounding air cools in temperature. Water vapor begins to stick to tiny particles in the air, such as dust. Clouds form when water vapor changes into liquid water droplets, which take shape around the tiny particles. Millions of these water droplets come together to form clouds high up in the sky. Eventually, rain or snow falls from the clouds, and water returns to Earth's surface.	For instance, Donatello's idea for lenticular clouds came on a random Tuesday as he was bouncing a rubber ball off his studio wall. The image for round discs of clouds in the sky just leapt into his brain. That afternoon, he hurried around his studio, molding and shaping this new cloud. He needed specific environmental conditions to make lenticular clouds. This new kind of cloud could only form when air gusted across mountains.

How Clouds Form	Donatello Stares at the Sky

Both

Directions: Reread "The Cloud." Then, respond to the prompt.

Imagine you are a cloud. Write a journal entry describing a day in your life as a cloud. Use the poem for inspiration.

_____
_____
_____
_____
_____
_____
_____
_____
_____
_____
_____
_____
_____
_____
_____
_____
_____
_____
_____
_____
_____
_____
_____
_____
_____
_____

Name: _____ **Date:** _____

Directions: Write a poem in response to "The Cloud" from the perspective of the wind, sun, or moon. Be sure to use figurative language and literary devices, such as rhyming, repetition, imagery, or alliteration.

_____

_____

_____

_____

_____

_____

_____

_____

_____

_____

_____

_____

_____

_____

_____

_____

_____

_____

_____

_____

_____

_____

_____

_____

Name: _____ **Date:** _____

Directions: Read the text, and answer the questions.

The Future of Cars

People around the world depend on different forms of transportation. Airplanes, bikes, and boats can all take people to and from destinations. But the most common form of transportation, especially in Asia, Europe, and North America, is the car. There are nearly 1.5 billion cars across the world! Automobiles, or cars, help people drive to work, school, the grocery store, and more.

Car technology may be due for some big changes. Climate change has led to many people reevaluating how they use and make cars. Cars will likely remain part of people's lifestyles, but the makes and models of those cars will likely change. Cars are shifting from being powered by gasoline to being powered by electricity. Cars are also likely to become autonomous, or self-driving, in the future. As new technology allows people to change how they use and make cars, it might not be long before we see a whole new line-up of cars on our roads.

1. How will climate change likely affect cars?
   - (A) It will have no effect.
   - (B) People will stop buying cars.
   - (C) Cars will be powered by electricity.
   - (D) People will buy more cars.

2. What is the main idea of this passage?
   - (A) Cars are necessary for modern life.
   - (B) Cars contribute to climate change.
   - (C) People will no longer need cars in the future.
   - (D) Cars will continue to change according to need and usage.

3. What is the tone of this passage?
   - (A) humorous
   - (C) informative
   - (B) persuasive
   - (D) critical

4. Which is a good antonym for the word *autonomous*?
   - (A) dependent
   - (C) strong
   - (B) alone
   - (D) capable

5. What kind of sentence is this? *Cars will likely remain part of people's lifestyles, but the makes and models of those cars will likely change.*
   - (A) simple
   - (B) compound
   - (C) complex
   - (D) compound-complex

Directions: Read the text, and answer the questions.

As You Read

Underline the environmental advantages of electric vehicles.

Going Electric

Long ago, cars used steam or electricity for power. This changed in the early 1900s. During this time, the gasoline engine was invented. Since then, the gasoline engine has been a reliable way to power cars. And gasoline has long been the go-to fuel for automobiles. However, many people are growing worried about the effect of vapors and gases released from gasoline engines. When gasoline is burned, it creates carbon dioxide. This greenhouse gas has contributed to climate change. Many people want to avoid making this problem worse.

Since the late 1990s, car makers have been building electric cars. Electric cars run using batteries that store electrical energy. Electric cars are known as zero-emission vehicles. They do not release vapors and gases like gasoline-powered cars. They are also more energy efficient. But, for now, electric cars usually cannot go as far as gasoline-powered cars. They can also take a long time to fully charge. They are often more expensive, too. For now, most cars on our roads are still gasoline-powered. But as electric cars gain in popularity, there may be a shift in the future.

1. True or false? Climate change has increased interest in electric vehicles.
   - (A) true
   - (B) false

2. According to the passage, why are people concerned about the use of gasoline fuel?
   - (A) the low cost of gasoline
   - (B) the effects of carbon dioxide
   - (C) the distance gasoline-powered cars can travel
   - (D) the time it takes to fuel up

3. Which is **not** a drawback of electric cars?
   - (A) limited driving distance
   - (B) can take a while to charge
   - (C) do not release carbon dioxide
   - (D) can be more expensive

4. Which is a good synonym for the word *emission* as it is used in this passage?
   - (A) absolution
   - (B) remittance
   - (C) relief
   - (D) discharge

5. What kind of connotation does the word *reliable* have?
   - (A) positive
   - (B) negative
   - (C) neutral
   - (D) none

6. Which line is the best evidence to support this statement? *Electric cars could be part of a solution for climate change.*
   - (A) Long ago, cars used steam or electricity for power.
   - (B) Electric cars do not release vapors and gases like gasoline-powered cars.
   - (C) For now, most cars on our roads are still gasoline-powered.
   - (D) However, many people are growing worried about the effect of vapors and gases released from gasoline engines.

Directions: Read the text, and answer the questions.

As You Read
Put a plus sign next to potential benefits of connected cars.

Getting Connected

People are increasingly connected to the internet. They use smart devices, such as smartphones, smart TVs, and smart watches. These devices help them stay connected to others. They also use these devices to connect to the internet for information and other services. Soon, cars may share this same kind of technology. These "connected" cars may represent the future of automobiles.

Using this internet connection, cars could then download crucial information about their surrounding environments. For instance, a connected car could sense heavy traffic conditions and slow down accordingly. A connected car could also "talk" to another vehicle and make safe driving decisions based on what the other vehicle does.

For now, cars rely on humans to guide and direct them. But in the future, a connected car would come directly linked to the internet. These cars would then use that connection to inform and change how they drive.

1. What would "connected" cars be connecting to?

  (A) the internet

  (B) information about traffic

  (C) other vehicles

  (D) all of the above

2. What might make connected cars safer?

  (A) They could access GPS systems.

  (B) They would be more efficient.

  (C) They would be able stop quickly when you press the brakes.

  (D) They could communicate with other cars.

3. Which is a good synonym for the word *heavy* as it is used in this text?

  (A) weighty

  (B) busy

  (C) viscous

  (D) trivial

4. Which of these words is used as an adverb in this passage?

  (A) accordingly

  (B) connected

  (C) crucial

  (D) slow

5. What can you conclude about the author's opinion on connected cars?

_____

_____

6. Would you like to drive a connected car? Why or why not?

_____

_____

_____

Driverless Technology

Self-driving cars might seem like a fun yet unrealistic daydream. However, in the future, it's likely most cars will be electric—and autonomous. For now, no cars are fully autonomous, or self-driving. Cars still require a human driver at the wheel. People need to keep their feet on the pedals, their hands on the wheel, and their eyes on the road. But in the future, self-driving cars will allow people to take their feet *off* the pedals, hands *off* the wheel, and eyes *off* the road. Autonomous cars will completely change the way humans drive.

The basics of some self-driving technology already exists today. For example, most cars have cruise control settings. Cruise control allows a driver to set a speed and take their foot off the gas pedal. The car then drives itself at the exact speed it is set to. Some cars also have settings that allow a driver to take their hands off the wheel. Using sensors, the car can adjust the steering automatically to help the driver park or maneuver through a traffic jam.

For a car to be fully autonomous, there needs to be technology that can replace human eyesight. Engineers are looking at how to add cameras and sensors to cars. This technology could then help cars see and respond to their surrounding environments. For

example, if a car can sense how close it is to the vehicle ahead of it, it can slow down. If a car can see a curve in the road ahead, it can turn its wheels to maneuver around the bend. A self-driving car needs this technology to safely navigate roads, traffic, and upcoming obstacles. This kind of car would need to be connected to the internet, too. This way, it would be able to take in information about the outside world. For instance, if it starts to rain outside, a self-driving car needs to sense this weather change and make navigation decisions accordingly.

So, why is there an emphasis on creating driverless technology? Part of the reason is that human error likely leads to more than 90 percent of all accidents on the road. Some people think the idea of driverless technology would remove the human element, which might make for safer driving. Self-driving cars would also make life easier for many people. Self-driving cars could drop someone off at work and pick them up at the end of the day. They wouldn't have to worry about a commute, and they could spend their travel time doing something else.

Fully autonomous cars are still far from reality. Driverless technology might be a part of our lives sooner rather than later, though!

Name: _____ Date: _____

Directions: Read "Driverless Technology." Then, answer the questions.

1. True or false? The author does **not** think that most cars in the future will be autonomous.

   (A) true   (B) false

2. What is responsible for the vast majority of car accidents?

   (A) poor signage
   (B) human error
   (C) faulty equipment
   (D) weather conditions

3. Which is a good synonym for *maneuver* as it is used in this text?

   (A) contrive   (C) avoid
   (B) scheme   (D) steer

4. How could driverless cars "see" the environment around them?

   (A) cameras and sensors
   (B) sonar
   (C) GPS
   (D) They could not.

5. Which of these could driverless cars **not** help with?

   (A) cost of building the cars
   (B) safety
   (C) tight parking spots
   (D) navigation

6. Record the pros and cons in the chart.

	Pros	Cons
Human-Driven Cars		
Driverless Cars		

Name: _____ **Date:** _____

Directions: Reread "Driverless Technology." Then, respond to the prompt.

> If driverless technology becomes the norm, should the regulations around driving change in any way? Consider the age and testing requirements. Write a persuasive speech outlining your reasons.

_____

_____

_____

_____

_____

_____

_____

_____

_____

_____

_____

_____

_____

_____

_____

_____

_____

_____

_____

_____

_____

_____

_____

_____

_____

_____

_____

Directions: Read the text, and answer the questions.

As You Read

Underline everything that Grand-peré says to Anthony.

When I Was Your Age...

It was only the second day of their road trip, and Anthony had already heard his grandfather start seven different sentences with, "When I was your age…" Anthony would never, *ever*, roll his eyes or disrespect Grand-pére. But really, it did seem like he was repeating the same sentence over and over!

"Anthony," started Grand-pere, "when I was your age, we never had these autonomous cars. I must say, I do not trust them."

Anthony sighed as he watched Grand-pére stare at the car's windshield suspiciously. Anthony's mom and dad had purchased a self-driving car a few years ago. Self-driving cars had been such a cool invention when they first came out. But now, the cars were everywhere, and they had lost their shiny sheen. Autonomous vehicles were just a normal part of daily life for everyone—except Grand-pére.

As Grand-pére had told Anthony many times, he grew up without social media, without a smartphone, *and* without a self-driving car. Anthony stared out the window as Grand-pére started wagging his finger at the car's dashboard. He thought to himself, *This is going to be a long drive.*

1. How does Anthony's grandfather feel about autonomous cars?

   (A) curious

   (B) wary

   (C) irate

   (D) credulous

2. Which word best categorizes Anthony's response to his grandfather's stories?

   (A) interest

   (B) annoyance

   (C) joy

   (D) debate

3. Which is closest to the meaning of *shiny sheen* as it is used in the text?

   (A) literal glow

   (B) new car smell

   (C) arrival

   (D) novelty

4. What is the best evidence to support this statement? *Anthony takes autonomous cars for granted.*

   (A) Anthony sighed as he watched Grand-pére stare at the car's windshield suspiciously.

   (B) Anthony's mom and dad had purchased a self-driving car a few years ago.

   (C) Autonomous vehicles were just a normal part of daily life for everyone—except Grand-pére.

   (D) He thought to himself, *This is going to be a long drive.*

5. Which word is used as an adverb in the text?

   (A) only   (C) self-driving

   (B) autonomous   (D) shiny

Name: _____ Date: _____

Directions: Read the text, and answer the questions.

As You Read

Underline words and phrases that show how Grand-pére feels about self-driving cars.

The 14th Birthday Road Trip

When every kid in Anthony's family turned 14, it was their turn to go on a seven-day road trip with Grand-pére. Grand-pére didn't live far from Anthony's house, so Anthony saw his grandfather often, usually at Friday night dinners. But it was one thing to hang out with Grand-pére at the dinner table with his parents, and it was a whole other thing to be one-on-one with him for seven full days!

Anthony's two older siblings laughed when they heard about this year's road trip. This was the first time Grand-pére had done a road trip in a self-driving car. Anthony's siblings had done the road trip in Grand-pére's old, electric pick-up truck. For years, Grand-pére had refused to get into a self-driving car. But this year, Anthony's parents had put their feet down. They told Grand-pére he needed to take their self-driving car for safety's sake. Grand-pére's eyesight was going a bit fuzzy, and Anthony's parents were insistent. The use of a self-driving car was the only way the birthday road trip could go ahead.

1. Why do Anthony's parents insist they take the self-driving car?
   - (A) It gets better mileage.
   - (B) It is faster.
   - (C) It is safer.
   - (D) It is newer.

2. Which of these words best describes the road trip with Grand-pére?
   - (A) tradition
   - (B) annual
   - (C) random
   - (D) loathed

3. How long is the road trip?
   - (A) two days
   - (B) a long weekend
   - (C) a week
   - (D) a month

4. What can you infer about Anthony and Grand-pére's relationship?
   - (A) They were estranged.
   - (B) They were well-acquainted.
   - (C) They were best friends.
   - (D) They did not get along.

5. Which is a good synonym for the word *insistent* as it is used in this passage?
   - (A) imperious
   - (B) halfhearted
   - (C) monotonous
   - (D) adamant

6. What kind of sentence is this? *Grand-pére didn't live far from Anthony's house, so Anthony saw his grandfather often, usually at Friday night dinners.*
   - (A) simple
   - (B) compound
   - (C) complex
   - (D) compound-complex

Directions: Read the text, and answer the questions.

As You Read
Underline the reasons why Anthony likes the self-driving car.

Where Are We Going?

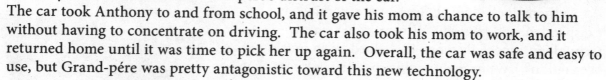

Anthony never knew where his siblings went on the infamous 14th birthday road trip. They refused to tell him, and they only mentioned that he'd love it and hate it all at once.

Anthony looked over at his grandfather, who occasionally touched the wheel of the self-driving car, muttering to himself. Anthony didn't understand Grand-pére's distrust of the car. The car took Anthony to and from school, and it gave his mom a chance to talk to him without having to concentrate on driving. The car also took his mom to work, and it returned home until it was time to pick her up again. Overall, the car was safe and easy to use, but Grand-pére was pretty antagonistic toward this new technology.

Anthony finally decided to ask where they were going to distract himself from his musings.

"Grand-pére, now will you tell me where we're going?"

Grand-pére's change in expression lit up the whole car, and he beamed at Anthony.

"We're going to my favorite place in the world—my cabin on Lake Michigan!"

1. What kind of connotation does the word *infamous* have?

   (A) positive
   (B) negative
   (C) neutral

2. Which is a good antonym for *antagonistic* as it is used in this text?

   (A) resentful
   (B) well-disposed
   (C) outgoing
   (D) objective

3. Why did Anthony ask where they were going?

   (A) He was dying to know.
   (B) He wanted to know when they would arrive.
   (C) He wanted a distraction.
   (D) He wanted to give his input.

4. What does the adverb *occasionally* modify in this sentence? *Anthony looked over at his grandfather, who occasionally touched the wheel of the self-driving car, muttering to himself.*

   (A) grandfather   (C) wheel
   (B) touched   (D) car

5. What are the reasons Anthony likes the car?

   _____

   _____

   _____

Name: _____ Date: _____

To Sit Quietly with You

There was no internet connection at Grand-pére's cabin on Lake Michigan. Anthony stood in horror as he tapped at his phone, trying in vain to get even one bar of service. Grand-pére chuckled as he watched Anthony fiercely try to connect to the outside world.

"That's the magic and beauty of this cabin, Anthony," Grand-pére said. "We are just outside of cellular range, and this cabin makes me feel like I'm back in the 80s again. We have no internet, no social media, no endless news! The only technology we have is that car outside."

Anthony looked up at Grand-pére, completely exasperated, and he said, "Why are you so anti-technology, especially when it's helped us so much? We couldn't have even done this road trip without that car. Someone else would've had to drive us up here, and that would've defeated the whole point of this trip."

Grand-pére stood silently, taking in what Anthony had said. He'd lit a fire in the cabin's main living space, and he motioned Anthony over to sit in a chair by the fire. The two sat in silence for a bit, and as the clock ticked on, Anthony felt himself settle down.

"You know, there's a quote from a French philosopher, Blaise Pascal, that I like," Grand-pére said quietly. "Pascal said, 'All of humanity's problems stem from man's inability to sit quietly in a room alone.' I do like technology, but you have to understand, sometimes things move fast, and I struggle to keep up."

Anthony nodded at Grand-pére, thinking of his struggles with the autonomous car.

"I try to keep up with all these changes, but I sometimes wonder if we lose something when we embrace or invent something new. Yes, I'll admit, that self-driving car made the trip up here so much easier—but there's a part of me, probably a prideful part, which wanted to drive you here myself without any help from technology."

"Why do you always bring us up here for this road trip, Grand-pére?" Anthony asked.

"I brought you up here to sit quietly in a room with you," Grand-pére replied with a smile. "I wanted to show you what my childhood was like without all the gadgets we have nowadays. I just wanted you to see what life was like for me back then. And I also like to take time to sit quietly in this room alone."

Anthony took in Grand-pére's words. "My mom told me once that every generation grows up with different expectations, knowledge, and hardships," he said. "She told me that you see the world through one lens, and I see it through another. She also said I could try harder to see things from your point of view."

Grand-pére smiled, and he reached over to pat Anthony on the back. "Well then, I'm very glad we've both decided to try seeing the world through each other's eyes."

Directions: Read "To Sit Quietly with You." Then, answer the questions.

1. Why is Anthony horrified?

(A) There is no internet at the cabin.

(B) There is no running water.

(C) The car has broken down.

(D) There is no television.

2. Which is the best synonym for the word *exasperated* as it is used in the third paragraph?

(A) amused

(B) frustrated

(C) exhausted

(D) placated

3. Which of these words best describes Grand-pére's attitude toward technology?

(A) excited

(B) bored

(C) conflicted

(D) indifferent

4. Which word best characterizes Grand-pére's attitude toward his own childhood?

(A) agitated

(B) nostalgic

(C) critical

(D) unsure

5. Which of these statements is **not** an opinion?

(A) I sometimes wonder if we lose something when we embrace or invent something new.

(B) There was no internet connection at Grand-pére's cabin on Lake Michigan.

(C) That's the magic and beauty of this cabin, Anthony.

(D) I also like to take time to sit quietly in this room alone.

6. What can you infer about Grand-pére's feelings toward Anthony?

(A) Anthony is his favorite grandchild.

(B) He only finds Anthony frustrating.

(C) He wants to share his views with Anthony.

(D) He thinks Anthony is smarter than him.

7. Compare and contrast Anthony's and Grand-pére's attitudes toward technology.

Anthony	Grand-pére
Both	

Name: _____ **Date:** _____

Directions: Reread "To Sit Quietly with You." Then, respond to the prompt.

Would you like to spend a week without internet or cellular connections? Why or why not? What would be most challenging and most rewarding parts for you?

_____

_____

_____

_____

_____

_____

_____

_____

_____

_____

_____

_____

_____

_____

_____

_____

_____

_____

_____

_____

_____

_____

_____

_____

FUTURE FEATURES OF CARS

Solar panels might line the rooftops of cars to help power them up in the future.

SOLAR PANELS

Some cars show information on their windshields to help drivers focus more intently on the road. Cars of the future could display information about weather conditions, road closures, or traffic.

HEADS-UP DISPLAY

In the future, cars might have computers in their dashboards which will display helpful information to drivers. This information might include directions to their next destination, speed limits, and potential hazards ahead.

AUGMENTED REALITY NAVIGATION

EXTERNAL AIRBAGS

Most cars already come equipped with internal airbags to protect drivers and passengers from harm in an accident. One day, cars might also have external airbags that could help prevent car accidents. Sensors outside might sense an upcoming collision. The airbags could then inflate, protecting and slowing down the cars.

ELECTRIC BATTERIES

Cars will likely say goodbye to fuel and instead power up using electric batteries.

Name: _____   Date: _____

Directions: Read "Future Features of Cars." Then, answer the questions.

1. What does the term *augmented* mean as it is used in this text?
   - (A) super
   - (B) diminished
   - (C) enhanced
   - (D) preserved

2. Which two words are close in meaning?
   - (A) *protecting* and *sensing*
   - (B) *data* and *information*
   - (C) *show* and *prevent*
   - (D) *limits* and *hazards*

3. Where would information appear on a heads-up display?
   - (A) the dashboard
   - (B) your phone
   - (C) the steering wheel
   - (D) the windshield

4. Which of these are ways that future cars might have enhanced safety?
   - (A) easier navigation
   - (B) real-time data about driving conditions
   - (C) sensors to prevent collisions
   - (D) all of the above

5. What kind of sentence is this? *Most cars already come equipped with internal airbags to protect drivers and passengers from harm in an accident.*
   - (A) simple
   - (B) compound
   - (C) complex
   - (D) compound-complex

6. What is the author's attitude toward the changes in future cars?
   - (A) disinterested   (C) confused
   - (B) excited   (D) objective

7. Sort the new features shown in the infographic into the correct category. Some may fit in more than one category.

Safety	Information	Efficiency

Directions: Closely read these excerpts, and study the infographic on page 167. Look for words and phrases that describe the influence of technology in positive and negative ways. Record the information in the chart.

Close-Reading Texts

Getting Connected	To Sit Quietly with You
People are increasingly connected to the internet. They use smart devices, such as smartphones, smart TVs, and smart watches. These devices help them stay connected to others. They also use these devices to connect to the internet for information and other services. Soon, cars may share this same kind of technology. These "connected" cars may represent the future of automobiles. Using this internet connection, cars could then download crucial information about their surrounding environments. For instance, a connected car could sense heavy traffic conditions and slow down accordingly. A connected car could also "talk" to another vehicle and make safe driving decisions based on what the other vehicle does. For now, cars rely on humans to guide and direct them. But in the future, a connected car would come directly linked to the internet. These cars would then use that connection to inform and change how they drive.	"You know, there's a quote from a French philosopher, Blaise Pascal, that I like," Grand-pére said quietly. "Pascal said, 'All of humanity's problems stem from man's inability to sit quietly in a room alone.' I do like technology, but you have to understand, sometimes things move fast, and I struggle to keep up." Anthony nodded at Grand-pére, thinking of his struggles with the autonomous car. "I try to keep up with all these changes, but I sometimes wonder if we lose something when we embrace or invent something new. Yes, I'll admit, that self-driving car made the trip up here so much easier—but there's a part of me, probably a prideful part, which wanted to drive you here myself without any help from technology."

	Positive	Negative
Getting Connected		
To Sit Quietly with You		
Future Features of Cars		

Name: _____ Date: _____

Directions: Closely read these excerpts. Compare and contrast the benefits of electric cars and self-driving cars as described. Then, answer the question.

Close-Reading Texts

Going Electric	Where Are We Going?
However, many people are growing worried about the effect of vapors and gases released from gasoline engines. When gasoline is burned, it creates carbon dioxide. This greenhouse gas has contributed to climate change. Many people want to avoid making this problem worse. Since the late 1990s, car makers have been building electric cars. Electric cars run using batteries that store electrical energy. Electric cars are known as zero-emission vehicles. They do not release vapors and gases like gasoline-powered cars. They are also more energy efficient. But, for now, electric cars usually cannot go as far as gasoline-powered cars. They can also take a long time to fully charge. They are often more expensive, too. For now, most cars on our roads are still gasoline-powered. But as electric cars gain in popularity, there may be a shift in the future.	Anthony looked over at his grandfather, who occasionally touched the wheel of the self-driving car, muttering to himself. Anthony didn't understand Grand-pére's distrust of the car. The car took Anthony to and from school, and it gave his mom a chance to talk to him without having to concentrate on driving. The car also took his mom to work, and it returned home until it was time to pick her up again. Overall, the car was safe and easy to use, but Grand-pére was pretty antagonistic toward this new technology.

Electric Cars   Self-Driving Cars

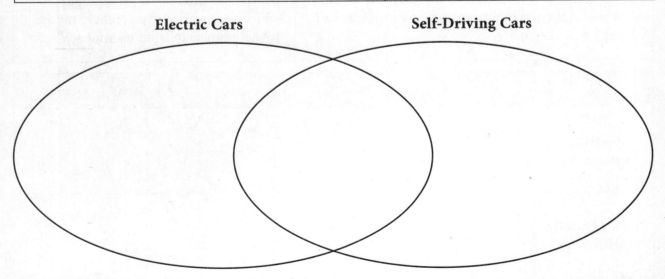

Which improvement is more important? Why?

_____

_____

Name: _____ **Date:** _____

Directions: Think about the texts from this unit. Then, respond to the prompt.

Imagine that you are Anthony from the story. Write a journal entry describing your time at the cabin with Grand-peré. What happened, and how do you feel about it? Be sure to include descriptive language to capture the experience.

_____
_____
_____
_____
_____
_____
_____
_____
_____
_____
_____
_____
_____
_____
_____
_____
_____
_____
_____
_____
_____
_____

Name: _____ Date: _____

Directions: Reread "Future Features of Cars." Think about another frequently used item that could be changed dramatically by adding new technology. Draw and annotate an infographic of that futurized item. Do not feel restricted by the practicality of the feature.

Directions: Read the text, and answer the questions.

As You Read
Underline definitions and statistics.

What Are Endangered Species?

Millions of plants and animals live on Earth. Scientists believe the planet is home to around 8.7 million species of living things. Many species thrive on the planet, but with human activity and climate change, some species have grown endangered. An endangered species is a species that is at a high risk of extinction. Extinction occurs when a living thing dies out and can no longer be found on the planet. There may be more than 41,000 endangered species on Earth. From red wolves to orangutans, there is a wide range of species in danger.

Species can be endangered at different levels. Some species can be endangered at a state level. Others are endangered at a federal or international level. In 1973, the U.S. Congress passed the Endangered Species Act (ESA). The ESA states that the federal government is responsible for protecting endangered species. The federal government has a list of endangered species. It can make special protections for species. For example, certain laws may be passed to prevent hunting. At all levels, people are interested in protecting endangered species.

1. Which is the best synonym for *thrive* as it is used in this text?
   - (A) deteriorate
   - (B) flourish
   - (C) survive
   - (D) decline

2. True or false? Most species on Earth are not endangered.
   - (A) true
   - (B) false

3. What kind of sentence is this? *From red wolves to orangutans, there is a wide range of species in danger.*
   - (A) simple   (C) complex
   - (B) compound   (D) compound-complex

4. What are the effects of the ESA?
   - (A) The U.S. Congress is required to protect endangered species.
   - (B) The government tracks which species are endangered.
   - (C) Endangered species are less likely to go extinct.
   - (D) all of the above

5. What can you infer about the U.S. government's attitude toward extinction?
   - (A) It is inevitable.
   - (B) It is unlikely.
   - (C) It should be prevented.
   - (D) It is not their concern.

Directions: Read the text, and answer the questions.

The Bald Eagle

Bald eagles have long been considered a national symbol of the United States. Bald eagles have a distinctive look. Their bodies are covered in a fluffy armor of brown plumage, and their heads are crowned with white feathers. However, only a few decades ago, bald eagles were considered an endangered species. In the 1960s, there were only around 500 bald eagles left in the United States.

Bald eagles were considered endangered for a few reasons. First, harmful pesticides were released into the environment at the time. These pesticides weakened the shells of bald eagle eggs. This led to the deaths of many young bald eagles. Humans also hunted the species. Other human activity, such as building development, led to the destruction of the eagles' habitats.

To reverse these effects, the U.S. government took action. The U.S. Endangered Species Act was created. It began offering special protections to bald eagles. Also, a ban on harmful pesticides was passed. Finally, captive breeding programs were put in place. While it took decades, the population of bald eagles in the United States recovered. In 2007, bald eagles were removed from the list of endangered species.

1. What was the most significant long-term effect on bald eagles of releasing harmful pesticides?
   - (A) The shells of their eggs were weakened.
   - (B) They went extinct.
   - (C) There was a ban on pesticides.
   - (D) They became endangered.

2. True or false? Humans were responsible for the decline in the population of bald eagles.
   - (A) true
   - (B) false

3. What is a good synonym for *armor* as it is used in this text?
   - (A) chain mail
   - (B) covering
   - (C) collection
   - (D) distribution

4. What does the suffix *–cide* mean in *pesticide*?
   - (A) removal
   - (B) chemical
   - (C) killing
   - (D) prevention

5. What is the best evidence for this statement? *The endangered species status is not a death sentence.*
   - (A) In the 1960s, there were only around 500 bald eagles left in America.
   - (B) In 2007, bald eagles were removed from the list of endangered species.
   - (C) This led to the death of many young bald eagles.
   - (D) It began offering special protections to bald eagles.

6. What is the author's purpose in writing this passage?
   - (A) to inform
   - (B) to amuse
   - (C) to persuade
   - (D) to critique

Name: _____ **Date:** _____

Directions: Read the text, and answer the questions.

As You Read

Underline facts about red wolves. Put stars next to the facts you find most interesting.

Red Wolves

The red wolf is a critically endangered species in the United States. Red wolves have reddish fur, live in packs, and communicate with howls, barks, and growls. In the past, red wolves roamed and hunted on the land between Texas and Pennsylvania. But human hunters and a loss of the red wolf's habitats led to a population decline. Today, red wolves can only be spotted in eastern North Carolina. They are the world's most endangered wolf.

Red wolf conservation efforts have faced challenges. For a period of time, red wolves were considered extinct in the wild. A captive breeding program helped bring back the species. But while some people believe this species needs care and protection, others see red wolves as a danger to livestock. As of 2022, around 250 red wolves are in captivity and under human care. Also, the U.S. Fish and Wildlife Service is developing a Red Wolf Recovery Program. Only time will tell if the red wolf population can thrive once again!

1. True or false? Everyone supports the protection of endangered species.

- (A) true
- (B) false

2. Which two words or phrases are used as antonyms in this text?

- (A) *endangered* and *dying out*
- (B) *spotted* and *conservation*
- (C) *captive* and *wild*
- (D) *challenges* and *hunted*

3. What can we infer about animals in captivity, compared to animals in the wild?

- (A) They are happier.
- (B) They are smaller.
- (C) They are sick more often.
- (D) They are easier to protect.

4. What kind of clause is this clause from the text? *For a period of time,*

- (A) dependent
- (B) independent

5. What are some challenges to protecting endangered species?

_____

_____

6. Do you think red wolves can be saved? Why or why not?

_____

_____

_____

_____

Name: _____ Date: _____

Is Conservation Important?

There are many endangered species in North America. The red wolf is just one example. There is also the burrowing owl, which is a species that makes its home in the Canadian prairies. This long-limbed owl saw a population decline when their grassland habitats were turned into fields for crops. Pesticides also killed the owl's food sources and affected the species' reproduction. Conservation agencies took steps to help, and the burrowing owl is now a protected species.

But why is the conservation of endangered species important? Some people argue that extinction is just part of nature. However, there is evidence that suggests the rate of extinction of various species is considerably higher compared to the past. Many vulnerable species are endangered due to habitat loss. Harmful pesticides in the environment have also led to population declines. Every species, including humans, lives in a diverse and complex ecosystem. Every living thing is connected to other living things. While it's impossible to predict the impact of one species going extinct, the loss could have a ripple effect. This is why conservation is so important.

Conservation is especially vital for keystone species. A keystone species can be any living thing, from animals to fungi. A keystone species is crucial to the survival of a habitat. If a keystone species is removed from an area, a chain reaction occurs. This reaction dramatically changes the biodiversity of the habitat.

Sea otters are one example of a keystone species. Sea otters are known for their playful energy, but they also serve a key role in their environment. Southern sea otters live in kelp forests near the coastlines of the Pacific Ocean. Kelp forests are critical to the health of this area's ecosystem. Sea urchins in the area love to eat kelp forests. Left unchecked, they can quickly devour a stretch of kelp forest with ease. However, sea otters like to eat the sea urchins that munch on the kelp. Sea otters help keep urchins from overeating the kelp. In turn, this maintains the health of kelp forests. But sea otters are considered an endangered species. For many years, fur traders hunted sea otters. Since 1977, sea otters have been listed as an endangered species. While their population numbers have climbed, they are still considered endangered.

People can make small, impactful decisions to help endangered species. For starters, they can look up endangered species in their local communities. They can see if there are ways to volunteer and help protect those species. They can also choose to not use harmful pesticides. Endangered species are in the most danger when they lose their habitats. Protecting their habitats protects them, too.

Directions: Read "Is Conservation Important?" Then, answer the questions.

1. What do the red wolf and the burrowing owl have in common?

- Ⓐ They are both from North America.
- Ⓑ They are both under protection.
- Ⓒ They were both harmed by human actions.
- Ⓓ all of the above

2. What does the prefix *bio–* mean in *biodiversity*?

- Ⓐ many
- Ⓑ life
- Ⓒ science
- Ⓓ brother

3. What is a synonym for *keystone* as it is used in the text?

- Ⓐ rocky
- Ⓑ large
- Ⓒ foundational
- Ⓓ unimportant

4. According to the text, why is it important to prevent extinction of any species?

- Ⓐ Loss of a species can affect the habitat of others.
- Ⓑ Loss of a species can affect the population of another species.
- Ⓒ There may be a chain reaction of negative effects.
- Ⓓ all of the above

5. Which word is used as an adverb in the text?

- Ⓐ impactful
- Ⓑ overeating
- Ⓒ impossible
- Ⓓ considerably

6. What is an example of a keystone species?

- Ⓐ red wolves
- Ⓑ sea urchins
- Ⓒ sea otters
- Ⓓ burrowing owls

7. Record the chain of events.

Fur traders hunt sea otters.
Sea otters become endangered.

Name: _____ **Date:** _____

Directions: Reread "Is Conservation Important?" Then, respond to the prompt.

Create a poster to inform and persuade people to take action to help endangered species. Use sea otters as an example. Be sure to use persuasive language and images to make your point.

Directions: Read the text, and answer the questions.

As You Read

Underline reasons why the narrator might want to visit China.

Our First Trip to China

The first time I ever left North America was on our first big trip to Asia. My mom had planned the trip for just the two of us so we could explore our heritage and culture together. My mom's mom came to America from China, while my dad's parents settled here from England. I'd grown up going to bilingual school, studying Mandarin in the morning and English in the afternoon. I knew enough Mandarin to say a few basic phrases, but not enough to feel confident ordering the correct dish off a menu. But when my mom asked me if I'd like to travel to China with her, I felt a tug to visit the country where my grandmother, my *wàipo*, grew up.

My mom and I travelled to China in early July, and as our plane soared over Hong Kong, I held my breath as I landed in a new country for the first time in my life. Over the next two weeks, we explored Hong Kong and Shanghai. We tasted wontons, milk tea, and egg tarts. We browsed markets and were jostled in the subways, and I found myself wide-eyed wherever we went. Finally, we arrived in Chengdu, the home of the giant pandas.

1. What can you infer about the narrator from the first sentence?
   - (A) They traveled to Asia again since this story.
   - (B) They moved to North America as a child.
   - (C) They did not want to go on the trip.
   - (D) They grew up in China.

2. Which is a good synonym for *jostled*?
   - (A) bullied
   - (B) bumped
   - (C) placed
   - (D) hurt

3. Which of these happened last?
   - (A) They flew over Hong Kong.
   - (B) They tasted many foods in China.
   - (C) They arrived in Chengdu.
   - (D) They planned a trip to explore their heritage.

4. What is the best evidence that the narrator's family values all parts of their heritage?
   - (A) *I knew enough Mandarin to say a few basic phrases, but not enough to feel confident ordering the correct dish off a menu.*
   - (B) *We tasted wontons, milk tea, and egg tarts.*
   - (C) *I'd grown up going to bilingual school, studying Mandarin in the morning and English in the afternoon.*
   - (D) *My mom's mom came to America from China, while my dad's parents settled here from England.*

5. Which word best describes the narrator's mood as they arrived in China?
   - (A) terrified
   - (B) eager
   - (C) weary
   - (D) concerned

6. Which word does **not** indicate sequence?
   - (A) first
   - (B) next
   - (C) finally
   - (D) with

Name: _____   Date: _____

Directions: Read the text, and answer the questions.

As You Read

Underline words and phrases that show how the narrator feels during the trip.

The Chengdu Research Base

When we arrived in Chengdu, I felt a bit exhausted from the ups and downs of travel. Hong Kong and Shanghai were a shock to my senses, as I'd spent most of my life in a sleepy small town. In both cities, there were so many people everywhere, crisscrossing the city at rapid paces. I stumbled over speaking Mandarin while my Mom practiced speaking Cantonese, another dialect. But somehow, we'd found our travel rhythms, and while I was tired, I could tell my mom and I were having fun.

We walked up to the Chengdu Panda Base, where, for the first time in my life, I would see a giant panda up close. Ever since I was a kid, I had dreamed of seeing a giant panda! My mom usually didn't buy me a costume for Halloween (we made them instead), but she relented one year and got me a panda costume. From that moment on, I read every book I could find about pandas, their idle habits, and how people were working to make sure they do not go extinct.

As we stepped up to the Panda Base, I felt my skin prickle with excitement.

1. Which word best describes how the narrator feels about meeting a giant panda?
   - (A) content
   - (B) elated
   - (C) jaded
   - (D) dispassionate

2. What element of the culture in China is most "shocking" to the narrator?
   - (A) the weather
   - (B) the food
   - (C) the scenery
   - (D) the crowds

3. What is a good synonym for *idle* as it is used in the second paragraph?
   - (A) lazy
   - (B) meaningful
   - (C) frivolous
   - (D) productive

4. Which of these words can be used as a verb, an adjective, and a noun?
   - (A) exhausted
   - (B) most
   - (C) close
   - (D) panda

5. Which of these characteristics is known about the narrator?
   - (A) age
   - (B) name
   - (C) gender
   - (D) interests

6. What happens first?
   - (A) They visit Shanghai.
   - (B) The narrator's mother buys a panda costume.
   - (C) The narrator reads every book about pandas.
   - (D) They land in Chengdu.

Directions: Read the text, and answer the questions.

As You Read
Underline facts about pandas.

A First Sighting

Lush, dense forest greeted us as we walked inside the Chengdu Panda Base. The base was built to be similar to a panda's natural habitat, so bamboo forests, caves, and rocks made up the environment. The base came together in 1987 when there were just six giant pandas here. That population grew with time and care, and now there are around 150 pandas that roam here at the base. I rattled off these statistics to my mom as we walked along the bamboo forests, and she smiled at me.

We'd arrived at the Panda Base right when it opened, since I had read online it was best to arrive as early as possible. The pandas were usually fed in the morning and fell asleep in the afternoons. I wanted to make sure I glimpsed at least a few pandas before they were napped out. As we walked, we rounded the corner to find the base's nursery house, and that is where I saw the first tiny, pink baby panda!

1. Which word is modified by the adjective *lush* in the first sentence?
   - (A) dense
   - (B) forest
   - (C) walked
   - (D) base

2. Which is closest to the meaning of *rattled off* as it is used in the text?
   - (A) flustered
   - (B) worked up
   - (C) listed
   - (D) informed

3. How would you describe the narrator's approach to visiting the panda base?
   - (A) spontaneous
   - (B) prepared
   - (C) haphazard
   - (D) casual

4. What usually happened in the afternoons?
   - (A) The visitors arrive.
   - (B) The sun grows too hot for the pandas.
   - (C) The pandas play.
   - (D) The pandas nap.

5. What does the narrator learn about these pandas before coming to the base?

_____
_____
_____
_____

6. Do you think the pandas that live at the base are happy? Why or why not?

_____
_____
_____
_____

As You Read

Underline words and phrases that show how the narrator feels during the visit. Circle words and phrases that show how the mother feels during the visit.

Me and the Giant Pandas

I had never seen such tiny creatures in my life! These baby pandas could fit in my hand. My mom and I pressed ourselves against the glass as we looked into the nursery, watching these babies who were only a week or two old greet the world. As I stared at them, I reflected on how soft and vulnerable the baby pandas looked.

"You were just as cute and adorable when I first met you," my mom whispered, nudging me.

After leaving the nursery room, my mom and I wandered around, moving fast but still taking our time to enjoy the whispers of the wind through the bamboo forests. We looked into one section and watched an older panda lie on his back, suntanning as he ate a piece of bamboo slowly, chewing with gusto. There were mothers nursing their babies, and there were pandas only a few months old climbing trees with slow, lanky limbs. I stared in wonder at a panda nicknamed "Dozy Dave" who laid on his side as he gazed up at the sky, perhaps daydreaming.

I'd seen pictures of pandas online, but I felt a huge sense of awe to see them with my own two eyes. I knew I was lucky to travel here with my mom, and I rapidly blinked my eyes, trying to take photographic memories to store away in my brain. I did not want to forget this precious moment in time.

"Did you know pandas are no longer considered an endangered species?" I asked my mom, who looked over at me with a wry grin and shook her head. "There are over 1,800 pandas in the wild. They're still a vulnerable species, but conservation efforts from a bunch of groups have boosted their population."

"That fills my heart up," replied my mom. "They are such peaceful creatures, and I hope they'll always have a home on our planet."

It seemed like the main goal of the base was to eventually release some of the pandas back to their wild habitats. That made sense to me, though I could also see how this massive base had become a home of sorts for these cuddly pandas, too.

As we continued to wander around, I thought about China and how the culture here was so different from my small hometown. Still, this country also felt like home to me as I learned more and more about my heritage. I started to think that perhaps there are many homes for all of us across the world, although my heart hoped the pandas would always have a home in the wild!

Directions: Read "Me and the Giant Pandas." Then, answer the questions.

1. Which is closest to the meaning of the phrase *with gusto*?

   (A) feebly

   (B) gently

   (C) enthusiastically

   (D) carelessly

2. What kind of sentence is this? *As I stared at them, I reflected on how soft and vulnerable the baby pandas looked.*

   (A) simple

   (B) compound

   (C) complex

   (D) compound-complex

3. Which word best describes the narrator?

   (A) idealistic   (C) bitter

   (B) casual   (D) inept

4. Which statement is the narrator most likely to agree with?

   (A) Vulnerable animals should be kept in captivity for the duration of their lives.

   (B) Animals should be returned to the wild when possible.

   (C) Attempts to keep animals contained are cruel.

   (D) Conservation of an endangered species is nearly impossible.

5. The narrator's overall impression of the panda base could best be described as what?

   (A) inspiring   (C) disappointing

   (B) ineffectual   (D) overwhelming

6. Consider the similarities and differences between the pandas in the wild and the pandas living at the base. Record the information in the chart.

Similarities	Differences

Name: _____ **Date:** _____

Directions: Reread "Me and the Giant Pandas." Then, respond to the prompt.

Create a promotional brochure for the Chengdu Panda Base, based on the information in the text. Include relevant text and pictures.

Meet the Orangutan

The world's largest arboreal mammal is the orangutan. Orangutans have a distinctive look, can use tools, and are in danger of dying out.

▶ *Orangutan* **translates to "person of the forest."**

Orangutans are apes that have long arms, coarse red fur, and gentle expressions. They are found only on the islands of Sumatra and Borneo. In Indonesian and Malaysian languages, *orangutan* translates to "person of the forest." These apes spend their lives above our heads, swinging from tree to tree in thick rainforests. Their days are split between resting and eating meals of ripe fruit. Scientists have found that orangutans have advanced cognitive abilities. They can recognize themselves in mirrors! Some orangutans can even use tools to forage for food. They are smart and capable animals.

There are three species of orangutans, and all are facing extinction. First, there is the Bornean orangutan. Then, there is the Sumatran orangutan. Finally, there is the Tapanuli orangutan. Both the Bornean and Sumatran orangutans are listed as critically endangered. The population of Bornean orangutans may have decreased by more than 50 percent since the 1970s. And there are likely fewer than 15,000 Sumatran orangutans. Researchers believe orangutans could face extinction in the near future. Their rainforest homes are quickly getting cut down. Trees are removed to make way for palm oil plantations. For Bornean orangutans, more than 80 percent of their habitat has been lost. Without meaningful change, orangutans may die out.

Name: _____   Date: _____

Directions: Read "Meet the Orangutan." Then, answer the questions.

1. Which of these is **not** a characteristic of orangutans?

   (A) red fur

   (B) long arms

   (C) silver backs

   (D) use of tools

2. True or false? Not all orangutans are critically endangered.

   (A) true   (B) false

3. The growth of which product is responsible for much of the orangutan habitat loss?

   (A) bananas   (C) kiwis

   (B) coffee   (D) palm oil

4. Which is a good synonym for *cognitive* as it is used in the first paragraph?

   (A) unintelligent

   (B) brain

   (C) heart

   (D) nimble

5. What is the tone of this article?

   (A) humorous

   (B) informative

   (C) critical

   (D) persuasive

6. Complete the graphic organizer based on the text.

New Information I Learned	Questions I Have about Orangutans

Name: _____ **Date:** _____

Directions: Closely read these excerpts, and study the article on page 185. Find and record evidence of why the animals have become endangered.

Close-Reading Texts

The Bald Eagle	Is Conservation Important?
However, only a few decades ago, bald eagles were considered an endangered species. In the 1960s, there were only around 500 bald eagles left in the United States. Bald eagles were considered endangered for a few reasons. First, harmful pesticides were released into the environment at the time. These pesticides weakened the shells of bald eagle eggs. This led to the deaths of many young bald eagles. Humans also hunted the species. Other human activity, such as building development, led to the destruction of the eagles' habitats.	There is also the burrowing owl, which is a species that makes its home in the Canadian prairies. This long-limbed owl saw a population decline when their grassland habitats were turned into fields for crops. Pesticides also killed the owl's food sources and affected the species' reproduction. Conservation agencies took steps to help, and the burrowing owl is now a protected species.

The Bald Eagle	Is Conservation Important?	Meet the Orangutan

Name: _____ Date: _____

Directions: Closely read these excerpts. Compare and contrast the ways in which the animals are described. Then, answer the question.

Close-Reading Texts

Me and the Giant Pandas	Meet the Orangutan
I had never seen such tiny creatures in my life! These baby pandas could fit in my hand. My mom and I pressed ourselves against the glass as we looked into the nursery, watching these babies who were only a week or two old greet the world. As I stared at them, I reflected on how soft and vulnerable the baby pandas looked. "You were just as cute and adorable when I first met you," my mom whispered, nudging me. After leaving the nursery room, my mom and I wandered around, moving fast but still taking our time to enjoy the whispers of the wind through the bamboo forests. We looked into one section and watched an older panda lie on his back, suntanning as he ate a piece of bamboo slowly, chewing with gusto. There were mothers nursing their babies, and there were pandas only a few months old climbing trees with slow, lanky limbs. I stared in wonder at a panda nicknamed "Dozy Dave" who laid on his side as he gazed up at the sky, perhaps daydreaming.	Orangutans are apes that have long arms, coarse red fur, and gentle expressions. They are found only on the islands of Sumatra and Borneo. In Indonesian and Malaysian languages, *orangutan* translates to "person of the forest." These apes spend their lives above our heads, swinging from tree to tree in thick rainforests. Their days are split between resting and eating meals of ripe fruit. Scientists have found that orangutans have advanced cognitive abilities. They can recognize themselves in mirrors! Some orangutans can even use tools to forage for food. They are smart and capable animals.

Pandas   Orangutans

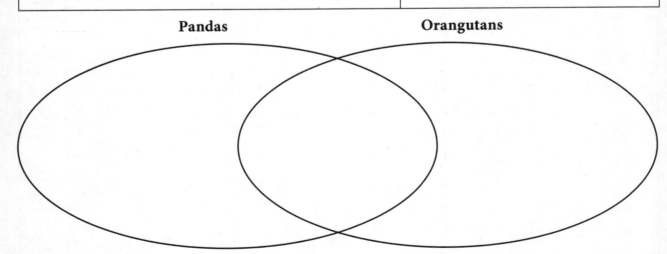

Do you think it's easier to get public sympathy for some endangered animals than for others? Why?

_____

_____

Directions: Reread "Meet the Orangutan." Then, respond to the prompt.

Write a poem in honor of the orangutan. Include specific details about the animal. Use at least one literary device, such as rhyming, repetition, alliteration, simile, or metaphor.

_____
_____
_____
_____
_____
_____
_____
_____
_____
_____
_____
_____
_____
_____
_____
_____
_____
_____
_____
_____
_____
_____

Name: _____ **Date:** _____

Directions: Select another endangered species. Research facts about that animal. Then, write a feature article in the style of "Meet the Orangutan." Include images and information about what makes that animal unique and why it has become endangered.

Name: _____ Date: _____

Directions: Read the text, and answer the questions.

As You Read
Circle adjectives used to describe buildings.

Iconic Buildings and Structures

Every major city across the world is home to iconic buildings and structures. These pieces of architecture can range from jaw-dropping skyscrapers to memorable music halls. The iconic buildings of a city often create a memorable skyline. A skyline is the outline of buildings against the backdrop of the sky.

One significant example is the city of Paris, which is the capital of France. If you were to think about Paris, one building that likely would come to mind is the Eiffel Tower. This is one of the most famous structures in the world. It stands tall in the heart of the city. This piece of architecture is a symbol for the city. It also draws a huge tourist crowd every year.

Iconic buildings and structures, such as the Eiffel Tower, leave an imprint on people's memories. These buildings and structures may be landmarks and can be historically significant. Examining the landmarks that define a city's skyline can also give insight into the values and culture of that area.

1. Why is the Eiffel tower important?

  Ⓐ It is famous.

  Ⓑ It is a symbol of Paris.

  Ⓒ Many tourists visit it.

  Ⓓ all of the above

2. What is a good synonym for *iconic* as it is used in this text?

  Ⓐ religious

  Ⓑ recognizable

  Ⓒ infamous

  Ⓓ tallest

3. True or false? Landmarks can represent values.

  Ⓐ true

  Ⓑ false

4. Which is the best synonym for *heart* as it is used in this text?

  Ⓐ emotion

  Ⓑ symbol

  Ⓒ center

  Ⓓ compassion

5. What kind of sentence is this? *Every major city across the world is home to iconic buildings and structures.*

  Ⓐ simple

  Ⓑ compound

  Ⓒ complex

  Ⓓ compound-complex

Name: _____   Date: _____

Directions: Read the text, and answer the questions.

As You Read

Underline physical descriptions of the Eiffel Tower. Circle emotional or symbolic descriptions.

The Eiffel Tower

The Eiffel Tower is the world's most recognizable metal tower. It was built between 1887 and 1889. Gustave Eiffel, a French engineer, was the architect behind the structure. The Eiffel Tower was first built as part of the Paris World's Fair. Originally, it was only supposed to have a 20-year lifespan. But Gustave Eiffel decided to design the tower to serve additional purposes. The tall structure has served as an observatory for astronomers. It has also been a communications tower and a lab for studying wind. Today, the Eiffel Tower is now a permanent part of Paris, and it has stood tall for more than 130 years.

Initially, many people were against the building of the tower. Some thought it would be a metallic eyesore. But as the tower rose during construction, people in Paris grew fond of its unique look. Part of the Eiffel Tower's appeal is also related to its height. It towers over nearby structures and is visible from multiple viewpoints. At night, the tower is eye-catching as it is lit up with twinkling lights. Through time, the Eiffel Tower has remained an iconic part of the Paris skyline.

1. Which of the following words best describes the usefulness of the Eiffel Tower over time?
   - (A) unclear
   - (B) versatile
   - (C) inflexible
   - (D) entertainment

2. Which word best describes the author's attitude toward the Eiffel Tower?
   - (A) surprise
   - (B) respect
   - (C) confusion
   - (D) unimpressed

3. Which is the meaning of *eyesore* as it is used in this text?
   - (A) ugly
   - (B) beautiful
   - (C) ocular
   - (D) inflamed

4. How do the people of Paris view the Eiffel Tower today?
   - (A) as something that should be hidden
   - (B) as something unique
   - (C) as a monstrosity
   - (D) as something mediocre

5. Which of these statements would the author likely agree with?
   - (A) The Eiffel Tower was surprisingly well-received.
   - (B) The Eiffel Tower was intentionally designed to be versatile.
   - (C) Gustave Eiffel should be proud of his accomplishment.
   - (D) all of the above

Name: _____ **Date:** _____

Directions: Read the text, and answer the questions.

As You Read
Underline what makes the Pyramids of Giza noteworthy.

The Pyramids of Giza

The Pyramids of Giza have been around for centuries. They were built during the height of the ancient Egyptian empire. The purpose of the pyramids was to serve as a final resting place for Egyptian kings. There are three main pyramids on the Giza plateau. Each pyramid was built for a single ruler. Smaller pyramids surround the main ones, and the Great Sphinx is found nearby. This large monument has the body of a lion with the head of man. This area is popular with tourists from around the world, and the pyramids have remained as iconic Egyptian structures.

The Pyramids of Giza are human-made structures. They are considered an extraordinary achievement in human engineering. Historians have spent countless hours researching the construction of the pyramids. But there are still mysteries as to how the pyramids were built without modern technology. Some historians believe workers built a raised bank or wall around the pyramid. The raised bank would have risen as construction continued. The workers might have moved blocks up the banks with ramps using levers.

Even after centuries of erosion, the Pyramids of Giza are still standing tall. Hopefully, these historical structures will stay protected for more centuries to come.

1. True or false? Scholars understand how the pyramids were built without modern technology.
   - (A) true
   - (B) false

2. What distinguishes the Pyramids of Giza from other iconic structures?
   - (A) their placement
   - (B) their age
   - (C) their materials
   - (D) their artwork

3. What is Giza?
   - (A) the ruler for whom the pyramids were built
   - (B) the river by the pyramids
   - (C) the plateau on which the pyramids were built
   - (D) the town 20 miles from the pyramids

4. Which is a good antonym for *extraordinary*?
   - (A) unusual
   - (B) mundane
   - (C) astonishing
   - (D) allowable

5. Summarize what makes the Pyramids of Giza noteworthy.

_____

_____

Name: _____   Date: _____

Modern-Day Wonders

Some iconic buildings and structures have stood tall for centuries. But many famous buildings have only been erected within the last hundred years. Some of these modern buildings have made strong impacts on their cities. This is especially true for a few music buildings that can be found around the world.

Sydney Opera House

First, the Sydney Opera House in Australia is an iconic performing arts center. It has a distinctive silhouette. From afar, the building looks as though it is made of three white seashells. Some people also compare the silhouette to white ocean waves. The building's creative design was seen as innovative and ahead of its time. The architect, Jørn Utzon, first sketched the plans in 1957. But the building required many more years of labor before its official opening. The building ended up severely over budget. Plus, Utzon abandoned the project before the opera house's doors even opened! Despite the controversy, the Sydney Opera House is now iconic and well-loved. It's a symbol for Australia. It is one of the country's best-known landmarks.

Elbphilharmonie Hamburg

Another building made for music and performances is Elbphilharmonie Hamburg. This concert hall was built in Germany, and it also finished late and over budget. The concert hall opened to the public in 2017. Since then, it's become an eye-catching and popular piece of architecture. The top half of the building is covered entirely in glass. The lower half is made of an old brick building that was once a warehouse. The concert hall's big draw is the main stage where 2,100 people can attend a musical performance. The seats surround the stage, and all visitors can enjoy an equally melodic experience.

A final iconic music building is the Harbin Opera House.

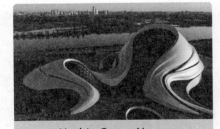
Harbin Opera House

Harbin was completed in 2015, and it lies in the northern part of China where winters are frigid. Harbin Opera House was built to blend in with the local wetlands and create a cultural centerpiece. The outside of the opera house sprawls with curves and whorls. Natural sunlight pours into the building through long, clear windows. Inside, wooden details create a warm atmosphere meant to mimic the inside of an instrument. The space is meant to evoke a warm, inviting haven from the cold and frost outside.

All three of these buildings are iconic pieces of architecture. The music, concerts, and arts events hosted in these buildings often bring people together and create a sense of unity. These buildings serve a purpose within their communities as centers for art and connection.

Name: _____ Date: _____

Directions: Read "Modern-Day Wonders." Then, answer the questions.

1. Which iconic structure was full of controversy during the construction period?

   (A) Harbin Opera House
   (B) Sydney Opera House
   (C) Elbphilharmonie Hamburg
   (D) none of the above

2. What is true about the Harbin Opera House?

   (A) The top half is all glass.
   (B) It mimics the movement of waves.
   (C) It is full of natural light and wood.
   (D) It can hold 2,100 people.

3. What kind of clause is this? *It's become an eye-catching and popular piece of architecture.*

   (A) dependent
   (B) independent

4. What do all three buildings have in common?

   (A) They have lots of natural wood.
   (B) They are of a similar size.
   (C) They host musical performances.
   (D) They were built in the 20th century.

5. Which building was built last?

   (A) Harbin Opera House
   (B) Sydney Opera House
   (C) Elbphilharmonie Hamburg

6. Which is a good synonym for *atmosphere* as it is used in paragraph 4?

   (A) troposphere
   (B) room
   (C) color scheme
   (D) ambiance

7. Record key information about each of the three buildings.

Building	Location	Unique Features

Name: _____   Date: _____

Directions: Reread "Modern-Day Wonders." Then, respond to the prompt.

> You have been hired to design a new performing arts center for your town. What do you want it to look like? Answer the questions, and draw a sketch of the building.

1. What kind of materials will you use?

_____

_____

_____

2. What shapes or images do you want to create on the outside?

_____

_____

_____

3. What kind of atmosphere do you want to create inside?

_____

_____

_____

Name: _____ **Date:** _____

Directions: Read the text, and answer the questions.

As You Read

Underline the jobs that Lewis Hine has held, and circle the subjects he has photographed.

Meet Lewis Hine

I ask you: do you know the influence of a photograph? I can still remember the first time I held a camera in my hands. There was so much power in looking through the lens and knowing I could capture a moment in time and share it with someone else.

But I, Lewis Hine, did not start my career as a photographer. In fact, I have worked all sorts of jobs. My first job earned me meager wages at a furniture upholstery factory. I eventually followed an academic path and became a geography teacher. I took my first photographs as a teacher, and it was then that I realized a photograph could become a tool for education. I snapped shots of my students as they bickered and chatted, and for the first time, I saw how someone could capture truth in a frame. You see, a photograph has the power to document a piece of history. And, some photographs have the power to *change* the course of history.

Since I picked up that first camera, I have never stopped taking photographs. I've documented the trials of immigrants who came through Ellis Island. I have taken photographs of children working in mills and factories under horrific conditions, and I even worked with the Red Cross during the Great War. But now, I am documenting something different. I am taking photographs of the construction of the Empire State Building.

1. In which point of view is this written?
   - (A) first person
   - (B) second person
   - (C) third person
   - (D) all of the above

2. What connotation does the word *meager* have?
   - (A) positive
   - (B) negative
   - (C) neutral

3. Which of these jobs did Lewis Hine **not** try?
   - (A) teacher
   - (B) photographer
   - (C) chef
   - (D) factory worker

4. What is a good synonym for the word *trials* as it is used in this sentence? *I've documented the trials of immigrants who came through Ellis Island.*
   - (A) ordeals
   - (B) assessments
   - (C) auditions
   - (D) arrivals

5. What is the best characterization for the kind of subjects Lewis Hine photographed before the Empire State Building?
   - (A) families
   - (B) celebrations
   - (C) struggles
   - (D) landscapes

Name: _____ **Date:** _____

Directions: Read the text, and answer the questions.

As You Read
Underline words and phrases that give context about what is happening in the world at this time.

The Tallest Building in the World

   A month ago, I was commissioned to document the construction of the tallest building in the world. The year is 1930, and as I walk through Manhattan, I can feel the tense fear and dread that line our streets. Last year, the stock market crashed, pulling down the dreams and hopes of so many people. When the men behind the Empire State Building asked if I would document the rise of the structure, I leapt at the opportunity. It is not wise to turn down work these days, especially when there are bills upon bills scattered across my desk. They have asked me to document the building's construction for publicity purposes. It's strange how, even with the world struggling, there is such excitement swirling around this new building.

   As I arrive at the construction site, passersby pause and stare. There is such an air of magic and intrigue surrounding the Empire State Building, something we've all felt such a lack of lately.

1. What is the meaning of the word *document* in this passage?
- (A) file papers on
- (B) record evidence of
- (C) watch carefully
- (D) question

2. According to the passage, what is one cause of the tense mood in Manhattan in 1930?
- (A) Major buildings had crashed.
- (B) There were too many people living there.
- (C) People had lost money in the stock market.
- (D) War was on the horizon.

3. What do people think about the construction of the Empire State Building?
- (A) a waste of money
- (B) uneventful
- (C) strange
- (D) thrilling

4. How does Lewis feel about the new job?
- (A) anticipation
- (B) unrest
- (C) turmoil
- (D) ambivalence

5. What kind of sentence is this? *Last year, the stock market crashed, pulling down the dreams and hopes of so many people.*
- (A) simple
- (B) compound
- (C) complex
- (D) compound-complex

6. What does the phrase *swirling around this new building* describe in this sentence? *It's strange how, even with the world struggling, there is such excitement swirling around this new building.*
- (A) world
- (B) strange
- (C) struggling
- (D) excitement

Name: _____ Date: _____

Directions: Read the text, and answer the questions.

As You Read
Underline the descriptions of what workers are doing.

The Sky Boys

During my first week on the job, I begin to take photographs of the "Sky Boys." Everyone calls them that because they are so high up! They are daredevils who casually walk across steel beams hanging high above the city streets. There are likely more than 3,000 workers on this project, raising this tall structure up one level at a time. Yesterday, I took a picture of a steelworker as he sat on a beam more than 1,200 feet (366 meters) in the air. It astounds me to think of the heights we are all working at!

I am constantly walking, trying to find the right angles to capture the personalities of the men working here. Some days, I hook myself to a safety line, take a deep breath, and walk to the ends of beams to get the shot I want. I have also started getting into a basket that swings from a beam overhead so I can get a better vantage point for my photographs. Who knew that at my age I'd be swinging in rickety baskets high above the streets of New York?

1. Why are the workers called the "Sky Boys"?
   - (A) They used to be pilots.
   - (B) The building is meant to look like a cloud.
   - (C) They work high in the air.
   - (D) They lift heavy beams as if they were made of air.

2. What is a good antonym for *daredevils*?
   - (A) showoffs
   - (C) cowards
   - (B) speculators
   - (D) gamblers

3. Which of these statements is true?
   - (A) Many of the workers seem nervous about the heights.
   - (B) Lewis is taking the same risks as the "Sky Boys."
   - (C) Lewis is only focused on capturing the progress of the building.
   - (D) Lewis always believed he would do this kind of job.

4. Describe Lewis's attitude and approach to the job.

   _____

   _____

   _____

   _____

   _____

Name: _____ Date: _____

Things That Had to Be Appreciated

My photographs from today are focused on the teams of men putting in rivets, which hold the steel beams of the Empire State Building together. Four men to a team are needed for the job. The first person works as a heater. They warm up the rivets and throw them to the second person, the catcher. The catcher catches the heated rivets in a paint can and uses tongs to then put them into a hole. The third person is the bucker-up, who holds the rivet with sturdy hands. Then, the fourth person, the gunman, hammers the rivet into place. Over and over, the heater, catcher, bucker-up, and gunman work in tandem. They work with only their hands and no harnesses, and there is such a quickness to their work. These men are determined to finish as much as they can in a day, and they take a lot of pride in how they are constructing this building.

As I looked through my lens today, I noticed how my camera trained on the men who dashed past me with rivets, hammers, and tongs in hand. All around us is economic uncertainty, but these men show up every day with dedication and exuberance. When I was hired for the job, they told me they wanted photographs of the building's architecture. My photographs will be used to publicize the building, I know. But secretly, I am taking photographs of the men who are creating this iconic building. While this building will be here for many decades to come, I know the men constructing this building will not be. History is here and gone in a heartbeat, and this is the deeper truth I hope to capture with my photographs.

When I return back home to my small apartment, I go through my negatives and hold some of my pictures to the light. I smile at these photographs of the men I now know so well. There's one of Joe carrying water to the workers and one of Carl napping on a beam, both set against the dramatic skyline of New York City. There is an imaginative, exuberant daring to the men who are constructing this building at such a quick rate.

Once, I talked to a reporter about my work: "There are two things I wanted to do: I wanted to show the things that had to be corrected. I wanted to show things that had to be appreciated."

Ultimately, I do not want the stories and work of these men behind the Empire State Building to be thrown into the dark, forgotten corners of history. But I know all I can do is take my photographs and hope that people will continue to see the things that need to be correct and the things that have to be appreciated.

Directions: Read "Things That Had to Be Appreciated." Then, answer the questions.

1. Which of these words is not used to describe the workers?

   (A) exuberance

   (B) daring

   (C) determined

   (D) averse

2. What is Lewis's overall goal on this job?

   (A) to record a remarkable building

   (B) to show the dangers of construction

   (C) to depict the workers who built it

   (D) to earn his money

3. What is significant about how the rivets are put in?

   (A) the cooperation and teamwork

   (B) the extra danger

   (C) the number of tools required

   (D) the ease of installation

4. What kind of sentence is this? *History is here and gone in a heartbeat, and this is the deeper truth I hope to capture with my photographs.*

   (A) simple

   (B) compound

   (C) complex

   (D) compound-complex

5. What does it mean to work *in tandem* as stated in this text?

   (A) in groups of two

   (B) together

   (C) in total

   (D) alone

6. Describe what each person does in the process of putting in the rivets.

Role	Task

Name: _____ **Date:** _____

Directions: Reread "Things That Had to Be Appreciated." Then, respond to the prompt.

Imagine you are hired as a construction worker to build the Empire State Building. The building is already half-finished when you begin. Write a journal entry describing your first day on the job. What did you do? What did you see? How was the experience? Draw what the building may look like after it is finished.

Greetings from Taj Mahal

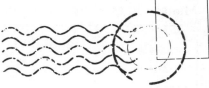

Greetings from Agra, India! I know you told me you didn't want me to send you anything, but I couldn't resist sending you a postcard from the Taj Mahal. We visited it as part of our 10-day tour today, and, Tasha, it looks exactly like this postcard! I've never seen architecture so picture-perfect against the blue backdrop of the sky. The Taj Mahal is a mausoleum, and it took around 17 years to build, with the finishing touches put on by 1648. A Mughal emperor, Shah Jahan, built it to honor and remember his favorite wife, Mumtaz Mahal. Mumtaz Mahal was the love of the emperor's life, and she was his most trusted confidant during their days together.

As I stared up at this mausoleum, I felt such a sense of awe of how a building can last through time. I also felt the magnitude of love present to build such a spectacular place. This is my first time traveling without your father, Tasha, and it has been a challenge in many ways. But being here makes me think of how I want to honor and remember him in my own life. I wanted to share that with you, and I cannot wait to see you when I'm back, my dear.

Love always, Mom

Tasha Dennings
123 Fox Street
Chicago, Illinois 60601

Name: _____ Date: _____

Directions: Read "Greetings from Taj Mahal." Then, answer the questions.

1. What is a good synonym for *mausoleum* as it is used in the text?

- (A) tomb
- (B) pyramid
- (C) building
- (D) museum

2. Which word best describes the author's attitude toward the Taj Mahal?

- (A) trepidation
- (B) approval
- (C) veneration
- (D) disdain

3. What kind of clause is this? *...with the finishing touches put on by 1648.*

- (A) dependent
- (B) independent

4. Which of these words is **not** used to describe the building?

- (A) picture-perfect
- (B) spectacular
- (C) incomplete
- (D) sense of awe

5. What is the meaning of *confidant*?

- (A) self-assured
- (B) employee
- (C) trusted person
- (D) greedy person

6. What is the theme of this postcard?

- (A) Appreciate the beauty around you.
- (B) Travel is healing.
- (C) Sharing experiences can help foster love and connection.
- (D) It's important to honor those you have loved and lost.

7. Think about the most impressive building you've ever seen. Compare and contrast the Taj Mahal and this building in terms of appearance and the overall impression they make.

Taj Mahal	Your Building
Both	

Name: _____   Date: _____

Directions: Closely read these excerpts, and study the postcard on page 203. Look for words and phrases that show how people see and respond to architecture.

Close-Reading Texts

The Eiffel Tower	The Tallest Building in the World
The Eiffel Tower was first built as part of the Paris World's Fair. Originally, it was only supposed to have a 20-year lifespan. But Gustave Eiffel decided to design the tower to serve additional purposes. The tall structure has served as an observatory for astronomers. It has also been a communications tower and a lab for studying wind. Today, the Eiffel Tower is now a permanent part of Paris, and it has stood tall for more than 130 years. Initially, many people were against the building of the tower. Some thought it would be a metallic eyesore. But as the tower rose during construction, people in Paris grew fond of its unique look. Part of the Eiffel Tower's appeal is also related to its height. It towers over nearby structures and is visible from multiple viewpoints. At night, the tower is eye-catching as it is lit up with twinkling lights. Through time, the Eiffel Tower has remained an iconic part of the Paris skyline.	A month ago, I was commissioned to document the construction of the tallest building in the world. The year is 1930, and as I walk through Manhattan, I can feel the tense fear and dread that line our streets. Last year, the stock market crashed, pulling down the dreams and hopes of so many people. When the men behind the Empire State Building asked if I would document the rise of the structure, I leapt at the opportunity. It is not wise to turn down work these days, especially when there are bills upon bills scattered across my desk. They have asked me to document the building's construction for publicity purposes. It's strange how, even with the world struggling, there is such excitement swirling around this new building. As I arrive at the construction site, passersby pause and stare. There is such an air of magic and intrigue surrounding the Empire State Building, something we've all felt such a lack of lately.

The Eiffel Tower	
The Tallest Building in the World	
Greetings from Taj Mahal	

Name: _____ **Date:** _____

Directions: Closely read these excerpts. Compare and contrast the descriptions of the people behind these iconic structures (either the workers or those who inspired the design).

Close-Reading Texts

Things That Had to Be Appreciated	Greetings from Taj Mahal
But secretly, I am taking photographs of the men who are creating this iconic building. While this building will be here for many decades to come, I know the men constructing this building will not be. History is here and gone in a heartbeat, and this is the deeper truth I hope to capture with my photographs. When I return back home to my small apartment, I go through my negatives and hold some of my pictures to the light. I smile at these photographs of the men I now know so well. There's one of Joe carrying water to the workers and one of Carl napping on a beam, both set against the dramatic skyline of New York City. There is an imaginative, exuberant daring to the men who are constructing this building at such a quick rate.	Greetings from Agra, India! I know you told me you didn't want me to send you anything, but I couldn't resist sending you a postcard from the Taj Mahal. We visited it as part of our 10-day tour today, and, Tasha, it looks exactly like this postcard! I've never seen architecture so picture-perfect against the blue backdrop of the sky. The Taj Mahal is a mausoleum, and it took around 17 years to build, with the finishing touches put on by 1648. A Mughal emperor, Shah Jahan, built it to honor and remember his favorite wife, Mumtaz Mahal. Mumtaz Mahal was the love of the emperor's life, and she was his most trusted confidant during their days together. As I stared up at this mausoleum, I felt such a sense of awe of how a building can last through time. I also felt the magnitude of love present to build such a spectacular place.

Empire State Building   **Taj Mahal**

Name: _____ **Date:** _____

Directions: Think about the texts from this unit. Then, respond to the prompt.

If someone were to construct a building to honor you after you are gone, what should it look like? Draw a picture, and describe the design and features. Explain why they would be meaningful for you.

Name: _____ Date: _____

Directions: Reread "Greetings from Taj Mahal." Research another famous landmark. It can be in your local community or on the other side of the world. Write and illustrate a postcard, describing what you see and why you think it is notable. Be sure to address your postcard to someone!

Directions: Read the text, and answer the questions.

As You Read

Circle the people and organizations who have gone into space. Underline the places they have gone.

Exploring Space

Most people spend their lives with their feet firmly planted on our planet. But for centuries, humans have been fascinated with what lies beyond Earth's atmosphere. In the last century alone, humans have made huge advances when it comes to space exploration. In 1961, Yuri Gagarin became the first human to enter space. Eight years later, Neil Armstrong took the first steps on the moon. Since those first forays, more than 600 people have travelled to space and spent time off our planet.

In the United States, the National Aeronautics and Space Administration (NASA) leads many space-related projects. Other private groups have emerged in recent years that are also launching space expeditions. Current space programs have put rovers on Mars and closely observed other planets in the solar system. But as technology continues to advance, more ambitious projects are in the works. In the coming years, NASA plans to send humans to the moon again. NASA and other private groups also hope to reach another ambitious goal—landing humans on Mars.

1. Which event came second?

- (A) Neil Armstrong walked on the moon.
- (B) NASA plans to send humans to Mars.
- (C) Private groups have started launching into space.
- (D) Yuri Gagarin was the first human in space.

2. What does the phrase *in the works* mean?

- (A) in the machine
- (B) causing trouble
- (C) stopped in its tracks
- (D) in process

3. True or false? In the United States, NASA is the only organization that sends up space expeditions.

- (A) true
- (B) false

4. *NASA* is an example of what?

- (A) haiku
- (B) onomatopoeia
- (C) acronym
- (D) initialism

5. What is a good synonym for *forays* as it is used in the text?

- (A) offers
- (B) ventures
- (C) assaults
- (D) volunteers

6. What is a good antonym for *private* as it is used in the text?

- (A) public
- (B) shared
- (C) clandestine
- (D) unrestricted

Name: _____   Date: _____

Directions: Read the text, and answer the questions.

As You Read

Underline planetary features that are similar to Earth. Circle those that are different.

Is Mars Next?

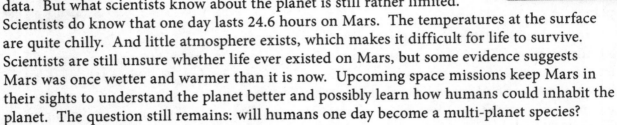

While Venus is the closest planet to Earth, most space expeditions have focused on getting to Mars. Venus has a burning-hot surface and stifling atmospheric pressure. Mars is farther away than Venus, but it offers some promising signs. Mars shares similarities with Earth, and some scientists believe Mars once had water and a thicker atmosphere. These factors could have led to a habitable planet.

NASA has already sent rovers to Mars to take photographs and collect data. But what scientists know about the planet is still rather limited. Scientists do know that one day lasts 24.6 hours on Mars. The temperatures at the surface are quite chilly. And little atmosphere exists, which makes it difficult for life to survive. Scientists are still unsure whether life ever existed on Mars, but some evidence suggests Mars was once wetter and warmer than it is now. Upcoming space missions keep Mars in their sights to understand the planet better and possibly learn how humans could inhabit the planet. The question still remains: will humans one day become a multi-planet species?

1. Why do most space expeditions focus on Mars instead of Venus?

   (A) Venus is too hot.
   (B) Mars has potential signs of life.
   (C) Mars is more similar to Earth.
   (D) all of the above

2. Which of the following is true about Mars?

   (A) The surface temperature is burning hot.
   (B) A day is close to the same length as on Earth.
   (C) It probably used to be colder than it is now.
   (D) It is closer to Earth than Venus.

3. What can you infer about the Earth's atmosphere based on the text?

   (A) It is similar to that on Mars.
   (B) It is thicker than that on Mars.
   (C) It used to be thicker.
   (D) It is similar to that on Venus.

4. What kind of sentence is this? *Little atmosphere exists, which makes it difficult for life to survive.*

   (A) simple
   (B) compound
   (C) complex
   (D) compound-complex

5. What is the author's purpose in writing this text?

   (A) to entertain   (C) to argue
   (B) to persuade   (D) to inform

6. What is the main idea of the second paragraph?

   (A) Mars and Venus are very different planets.
   (B) Mars is a lot like Earth.
   (C) Scientists want to study Mars to look for signs of life or the potential for it.
   (D) Scientists want to understand why Mars is so cold.

Directions: Read the text, and answer the questions.

Put a plus sign next to the benefits of the ISS.

The International Space Station

Space exploration has many benefits to humankind. One benefit is that it invites cooperation among different nations. One example is the International Space Station (ISS) that orbits Earth. It is a home for laboratories in space. From 1998 to 2011, multiple countries helped build it. The United States first put together the plans for the ISS, but the station only came together with the help of five other space agencies. Since 2000, there has always been a crew on board the ISS. Historically, the crew is made up of people from across the globe.

The research conducted on the ISS has led to many meaningful benefits for people on Earth. Some research done on the ISS has led to improved CT scans. This is a kind of medical scanning technology. The astronauts who live on the ISS also run experiments in microgravity. Over time, people have learned more about microgravity thanks in part to the work done on the ISS. The astronauts on board always work together to research and learn new things.

1. What is the purpose of the ISS?
   (A) to conduct research in space
   (B) to develop better space ships
   (C) to build better weapons
   (D) to protect Earth from space attacks

2. How many space agencies were involved in creating the ISS?
   (A) one
   (B) two
   (C) five
   (D) six

3. What is the main idea of this passage?
   (A) The ISS was built by many nations.
   (B) The ISS is a great accomplishment of the United States.
   (C) Experiments are conducted on the ISS.
   (D) The ISS benefits everyone through its research and cooperation.

4 What is a good synonym for *meaningful* as it is used in the text?
   (A) evocative   (C) futile
   (B) significant   (D) trivial

5. What examples are given of the benefits of the ISS?

_____
_____
_____

6. Do you think it's important that the ISS is a multi-national effort? Why or why not?

_____
_____

© Shell Education   135158—180 Days of Reading   211

As You Read
Underline information you already knew. Put a star next to information that is new to you.

Why Explore Space?

Human curiosity about outer space has led to people exploring and experimenting with new ways of going beyond Earth's atmosphere. But space missions take considerable planning to execute. There's no ignoring the fact that space exploration also comes with a high price tag. Large budgets and countless years are needed to keep sending technology and people into space. So, why do people still want to explore past Earth's atmosphere?

For starters, space exploration has helped improve life on Earth in surprising ways. Space exploration has led to helpful technology research and advancement. People have created innovative strategies that allow astronauts to explore space safely. This has led to a number of inventions that people still use today. One example is freeze-dried food, which is a necessity in space. Those freeze-dried meals can also be found in camping backpacks. Another example is the foil blanket. In the 1960s, scientists created a plastic blanket lined with a metallic substance for space travel. This foil blanket reflected body heat back to a person. These foil blankets are now a regular sight in medical kits. They are often used to keep people warm if they've gone through a shock or completed a marathon. Other inventions that were created with the help of space programs include cameras on phones and LED lights. People also have space programs to thank for memory foam, wireless headsets, and so much more.

Another possible reason to keep funding space programs is so Earth can dodge a disastrous date with an asteroid. Some space programs are exploring how to redirect an asteroid if one were to come our way. Scientists believe that long ago, an asteroid collided with the planet. It caused the extinction of dinosaurs. Some people want to prevent the same thing from happening to humans. There are currently no asteroids on a collision path with Earth, but it doesn't hurt to be prepared!

Some people point out that space mining and inhabiting another planet are also compelling reasons to keep exploring space. Some people believe space mining would give humans access to new natural resources. These resources could be used to create new things on Earth. Some people also suggest that it's crucial to explore building homes on other planets, such as Mars. This would be useful in case Earth becomes inhospitable for human life.

There are many reasons to continue to explore space. Perhaps the final reason that keeps people curious about space is that humans are explorers at heart. People love seeing new places and learning about the world around them. Exploring space may also inspire younger generations. When young adults see people do something that once seemed impossible, it encourages them to keep dreaming big. Space can offer a frontier for people to be creative and innovative together.

Directions: Read "Why Explore Space?" Then, answer the questions.

1. What are some of the obstacles to successful space expeditions?

    Ⓐ time

    Ⓑ difficulty of planning

    Ⓒ high cost

    Ⓓ all of the above

2. Based on this text, what can you conclude about innovations such as freeze-dried food?

    Ⓐ They have limited uses.

    Ⓑ They have unexpected benefits.

    Ⓒ They are fun but not necessary.

    Ⓓ They were easy to develop.

3. What can you infer about the repetition of the word *some* in the second-to-last paragraph?

    Ⓐ These are the results of research by individuals.

    Ⓑ These ideas are shared anonymously.

    Ⓒ These are opinions that are not universally shared.

    Ⓓ No one can believe in more than one of those ideas.

4. Which of these statements is an opinion?

    Ⓐ People also have space programs to thank for memory foam, wireless headsets, and so much more.

    Ⓑ Large budgets and countless years are needed to keep sending technology and people into space.

    Ⓒ These foil blankets are now a regular sight in medical kits.

    Ⓓ Perhaps the final reason that keeps people curious about space is that humans are explorers at heart.

5. Which of these inventions was developed through space research?

    Ⓐ LED lights

    Ⓑ computers

    Ⓒ cereal

    Ⓓ down comforters

6. Record the benefits of space exploration we enjoy today and those that might be possible in the future.

Benefits for the Present	Benefits for the Future

Name: _____ Date: _____

Directions: Reread "Why Explore Space?" Then, respond to the prompt.

Imagine that people want to stop funding space exploration. Write a speech to explain the most important reasons why we should continue to fund space expeditions and research. Be specific and persuasive in your language.

_____

_____

_____

_____

_____

_____

_____

_____

_____

_____

_____

_____

_____

_____

_____

_____

_____

_____

_____

_____

_____

_____

Directions: Read the text, and answer the questions.

As You Read
Underline physical descriptions of the Space Station.

Talia's New Home

From: taliabrown@fauxmail.com
To: brown_family@fauxmail.com
Subject: Miss y'all

Dear family,

Thank you for all your questions—it does make me feel missed and appreciated! I'm finally starting to settle into the rhythms and routines of being here at the International Space Station. Even though I have spent years preparing to be here, it does take a bit of time to settle in.

Mya, you asked for a rough layout of the station, so I'll do my best to sketch you a picture with my words. The space station is long and narrow, and there are six bunks for us, as well as a handy gym. We have to work out for at least two hours a day here or else we lose too much muscle mass. (I don't use my lower body muscles to walk around up here because of microgravity.) There's also a massive viewing window that allows us to spin in a circle and see the surrounding 'space.' Oh yes, and there are laboratories for us to conduct our experiments, which is arguably the whole reason why we are here.

More soon,

Your Talia

1. What kind of format is this writing?
   - (A) journal entry
   - (B) letter
   - (C) email
   - (D) text message

2. Why is exercise important on the Space Station?
   - (A) There's not much else to do.
   - (B) A lot of food is consumed.
   - (C) Muscles don't get used in low gravity.
   - (D) Strength is required for the work.

3. Which word is used as an adverb in the text?
   - (A) missed
   - (B) handy
   - (C) massive
   - (D) arguably

4. What is the best evidence to support this statement? *Living on the International Space Station takes some getting used to.*
   - (A) The space station is long and narrow, and there are six bunks for us, as well as a handy gym.
   - (B) Even though I have spent years preparing to be here, it does take a bit of time to settle in.
   - (C) We have to work out for at least two hours a day here or else we lose too much muscle mass.
   - (D) Oh yes, and there are laboratories for us to conduct our experiments, which is arguably the whole reason why we are here.

Name: _____ Date: _____

Directions: Read the text, and answer the questions.

As You Read
Underline information you find surprising.

An Astronaut's Menu

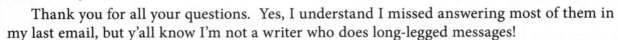

From: taliabrown@fauxmail.com

To: brown_family@fauxmail.com

Subject: Yes, I'm Eating

Dear family,

Thank you for all your questions. Yes, I understand I missed answering most of them in my last email, but y'all know I'm not a writer who does long-legged messages!

Mom, that's right, there is no refrigerator here at the station, so everything I eat comes out of a vacuum-packed bag. Sometimes I add water to liven up a package of spaghetti, but my favorite is our bags of scrambled eggs—*kidding.* (As y'all know, I still have an ever-persistent fear of eggs in any shape or form.) Making a meal is always a laugh here because I need to tape down my ingredients to the table so they don't float off. When I eat with my crew, we strap our trays to our laps or the wall because if we didn't, those would just float away, too!

Yes, I was allowed to choose a variety of foods before we left, and I did request peanut butter and brownies before we took off, because, well—priorities.

More soon,

Your Talia

1. What is the style of writing in these messages?

   (A) formal   (B) informal

2. How does Talia's mood sound in this message?

   (A) humorous   (C) anxious

   (B) lonely   (D) serious

3. What kind of sentence is this? *Yes, I was allowed to choose a variety of foods before we left, and I did request peanut butter and brownies before we took off, because, well—priorities.*

   (A) simple

   (B) compound

   (C) complex

   (D) compound-complex

4. What can you infer from the second sentence?

   (A) Talia's family is not interested in her trip.

   (B) Talia's family was content with her first message.

   (C) Talia's family was impatient to hear her answers.

   (D) Talia's family did not expect a long reply.

5. Why is all the food vacuum-packed?

   (A) It is cheaper.

   (B) It is tastier.

   (C) There is no water on board.

   (D) There is no refrigerator.

6. What does Talia mean by *long-legged messages*?

   (A) fancy messages   (C) short messages

   (B) wordy messages   (D) messages about herself

Directions: Read the text, and answer the questions.

As You Read

Underline text that indicates that Talia is having a hard time.

Answers to 28 Emails

From: taliabrown@fauxmail.com

To: brown_family@fauxmail.com

Subject: Vague Answers to 28 Emails

Dear family,

Thank you for all (28) emails you sent yesterday. I did take time to read them all, and, no, I'm not ignoring your questions, Mya. You know you are my favorite niece, but really— you pack questions into an email like sardines into a can!

Okay, here are some rapid-fire answers for your inquisitive emails. Yes, I still wash my hair often (I stay clean, okay), but I use this "rinse-less" shampoo that can stick around in my hair. Yes, I sleep in a little cabin bunk every day, and I have to strap myself down so I don't float away while dreaming! Yes, I still drink coffee every day, even though I cannot pair it with Mama's famous waffles.

I've been at the station for nearly a month, and there are two other crew members here with me. So, I don't have a ton of time where I'm truly alone or feel lonely, but still—I miss having you lot all around me for Sunday barbeques and chats on the front porch. But I am so grateful to be up here in the sky, and it's hard to describe how beautiful Earth looks from this vantage point!

More soon,

Your Talia

1. What is the most likely reason that Talia never answers all her family's questions?

   Ⓐ She is not very close to her family.

   Ⓑ She doesn't like to type.

   Ⓒ She is very busy.

   Ⓓ She would rather nap.

2. What is the best description of Talia's attitude toward this opportunity?

   Ⓐ appreciative   Ⓒ dutiful

   Ⓑ tolerant   Ⓓ despondent

3. What kind of literary device is used in this sentence? *...you pack questions into an email like sardines into a can!*

   Ⓐ hyperbole   Ⓒ metaphor

   Ⓑ simile   Ⓓ repetition

4. What is a good synonym for *vantage point*?

   Ⓐ window   Ⓒ perspective

   Ⓑ image   Ⓓ sight

5. Do you think Talia is close to her family? What evidence can you cite from the text?

   _____

   _____

Name: _____   Date: _____

As You Read
Underline each activity Talia engages in on a typical day.

Meaningful Work

From: taliabrown@fauxmail.com

To: brown_family@fauxmail.com

Subject: A Day in My Life, As Requested by Mya

Dear family,

It is Sunday here, and as y'all know, I have my weekends free. I thought I'd give y'all a small glimpse at what a work day looks like for me, especially since everyone is so full of questions.

To begin with, every day looks different for me up here at the space station. Some days I'm conducting experiments, and on others, I am fixing something that's gone belly-up. Usually though, I am up around six in the morning, which is when I look through my to-dos and general schedule. There are some tasks I can do at any time of day, but for other tasks, I need to coordinate with the team on the ground.

I do spend over two hours every day exercising. I use a resistance machine that helps me "lift" weights, and this is how I stay strong and healthy. Mama, you asked how long my work days are, and they are longer than on Earth; I have one hour for lunch, and another eleven hours go toward my work tasks and exercising.

Mya, thanks so much for worrying about me and my "lonely self." Here's the thing: for as long as I can remember, I have wanted to become an astronaut. But when we say *yes* to one dream, we are often saying *no* to something else. And when I said *yes* to my dream of being in space, that meant I was letting go of some precious time with y'all back home. I know we have email and our usual phone chats, but yes, I do feel far away from you.

However, it is easier to embrace a bit of loneliness because I know what I am doing up here matters. For instance, this week, I tended to the plants we have growing in our laboratory. Our red romaine lettuce is looking especially well, and I have faith that many of our experiments will help people back home in some way, even though some of them might not work out. Like Mama is always saying, our actions have a ripple effect that extend outward from ourselves. I want to live my life doing things that will hopefully help others. When I help others, I feel like I am doing something meaningful—and that's important to me.

I also want y'all to know how meaningful your emails are to me and how they touch my heart. At the end of the day, we all want to know we are loved, and I feel so loved when I read all 37 of your emails from any given day. I'll be home before you know it, and until then, thank you for keeping me in your hearts!

More soon,

Your Talia

Name: _____ **Date:** _____

Directions: Read "Meaningful Work." Then, answer the questions.

1. What is the meaning of the phrase *gone belly-up* in the second paragraph?
   - (A) relaxed
   - (B) gotten stretched
   - (C) lost weight
   - (D) stopped working

2. What helps Talia deal with the loneliness?
   - (A) her salary
   - (B) the different views of space
   - (C) her meaningful work
   - (D) her weekends off

3. What is a good antonym for *embrace* as it is used in the text?
   - (A) accept
   - (B) squeeze
   - (C) reject
   - (D) incorporate

4. Which of these words indicates contrast?
   - (A) many
   - (B) however
   - (C) like
   - (D) also

5. What kind of clause is this? *...especially since everyone is so full of questions*
   - (A) dependent
   - (B) independent

6. Using the information in the text, create a sample daily schedule for Talia for a weekday at the space station.

Time	Activity

Name: _____   **Date:** _____

Directions: Reread "Meaningful Work." Then, respond to the prompt.

Imagine you are Talia. Write a journal entry dated the week after you return to Earth. What are you most excited to see and do again on Earth? What do you miss most about being on the space station?

_____
_____
_____
_____
_____
_____
_____
_____
_____
_____
_____
_____
_____
_____
_____
_____
_____
_____
_____
_____
_____
_____
_____

WOMEN IN SPACE

NASA's missions depend on creative and thoughtful perspectives. People who work for NASA need to solve problems and come up with innovative solutions. According to NASA, diversity drives innovation. This is why NASA hires astronauts, engineers, and leaders from a variety of backgrounds. However, while more than 600 people have gone into space, fewer than 100 have been women. Here's a timeline of key dates for women in space.

JULY 1958
NASA is established.

JUNE 1963
Valentina Tereshkova becomes the first woman to go to space.

JANUARY 1978
NASA selects 35 new astronauts for its Space Shuttle Program. For the first time, six women are included in the program.

JUNE 1983
Sally Ride becomes the first American woman in space.

SEPTEMBER 1992
Mae Jemison becomes first Black woman in space.

APRIL 1993
Ellen Ochoa becomes the first Hispanic woman in space. She later becomes the director of NASA's Johnson Space Center.

APRIL 2008
Peggy Whitson becomes the first female space station commander as she takes the helm of the International Space Station.

SEPTEMBER 2017
Peggy Whitson returns from her last foray into space. She officially becomes the astronaut with the most total time in space. She spent 665 days, 22 hours, and 22 minutes in orbit!

OCTOBER 2019
Christina Koch and Jessica Meir go on the first all-female spacewalk.

Name: _____ **Date:** _____

Directions: Read "Women in Space." Then, answer the questions.

1. True or false? Valentine Tereshkova was American.

   Ⓐ true   Ⓑ false

2. Which event happened first?

   Ⓐ The first female space station commander was appointed.

   Ⓑ NASA chose Ellen Ochoa as the director of the Johnson Space Center.

   Ⓒ The first Black woman went into space.

   Ⓓ The first American woman went into space.

3. True or false? Peggy Whitson has spent more time in space than any man.

   Ⓐ true   Ⓑ false

4. Approximately what fraction of American astronauts have been women?

   Ⓐ $\frac{1}{2}$

   Ⓑ $\frac{1}{3}$

   Ⓒ $\frac{1}{4}$

   Ⓓ $\frac{1}{6}$

5. Approximately how many years did it take from the start of NASA to the appointment of the first American women astronauts?

   Ⓐ 5 years

   Ⓑ 10 years

   Ⓒ 20 years

   Ⓓ 30 years

6. Which event from the time line do you think is most significant? Why?

   _____

   _____

   _____

   _____

   _____

   _____

135158—180 Days of Reading

Name: _____   **Date:** _____

Directions: Closely read these excerpts, and study the time line on page 221. Record words and phrases that describe the purpose or benefit of space exploration.

Close-Reading Texts

The International Space Station	Meaningful Work
Space exploration has many benefits to humankind. One benefit is that it invites cooperation among different nations. One example is the International Space Station (ISS) that orbits Earth. It is a home for laboratories in space. From 1998 to 2011, multiple countries helped build it. The United States first put together the plans for the ISS, but the station only came together with the help of five other space agencies. Since 2000, there has always been a crew on board the ISS. Historically, the crew is made up of people from across the globe.	However, it is easier to embrace a bit of loneliness because I know what I am doing up here matters. For instance, this week, I tended to the plants we have growing in our laboratory. Our red romaine lettuce is looking especially well, and I have faith that many of our experiments will help people back home in some way, even though some of them might not work out. Like Mama is always saying, our actions have a ripple effect that extend outward from ourselves. I want to live my life doing things that will hopefully help others. When I help others, I feel like I am doing something meaningful—and that's important to me.

Text	Purpose or Benefit
The International Space Station	
Meaningful Work	
Women in Space	

Name: _____ **Date:** _____

Directions: Closely read these excerpts. Then, compare and contrast how they describe the challenges of living in space and the solutions that have been found.

Close-Reading Texts

Why Explore Space?	Answers to 28 Emails
People have created innovative strategies that allow astronauts to explore space safely. This has led to a number of inventions that people still use today. One example is freeze-dried food, which is a necessity in space. Those freeze-dried meals can also be found in camping backpacks. Another example is the foil blanket. In the 1960s, scientists created a plastic blanket lined with a metallic substance for space travel. This foil blanket reflected body heat back to a person. These foil blankets are now a regular sight in medical kits. They are often used to keep people warm if they've gone through a shock or completed a marathon.	Okay, here are some rapid-fire answers for your inquisitive emails. Yes, I still wash my hair often (I stay clean, okay), but I use this "rinse-less" shampoo that can stick around in my hair. Yes, I sleep in a little cabin bunk every day, and I have to strap myself down so I don't float away while dreaming! Yes, I still drink coffee every day, even though I cannot pair it with Mama's famous waffles. I've been at the station for nearly a month, and there are two other crew members here with me. So, I don't have a ton of time where I'm truly alone or feel lonely, but still—I miss having you lot all around me for Sunday barbeques and chats on the front porch. But I am so grateful to be up here in the sky, and it's hard to describe how beautiful Earth looks from this vantage point!

Why Explore Space?   Answers to 28 Emails

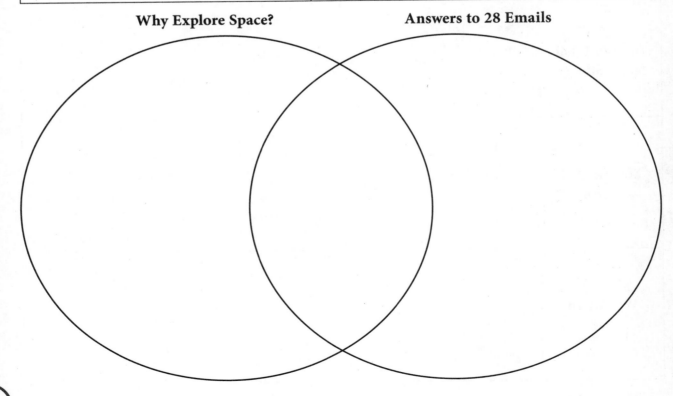

Name: _____ **Date:** _____

Directions: Think about the texts from this unit. Then, respond to the prompt.

Is space exploration worth the massive investment of time and resources? Write a letter to the editor of a newspaper, explaining your opinion and your reasons.

_____
_____
_____
_____
_____
_____
_____
_____
_____
_____
_____
_____
_____
_____
_____
_____
_____
_____
_____
_____
_____
_____
_____

Name: _____ Date: _____

Directions: Research one of the recent private companies that is sending expeditions into space. Create a time line of their activities, with a brief description of each.

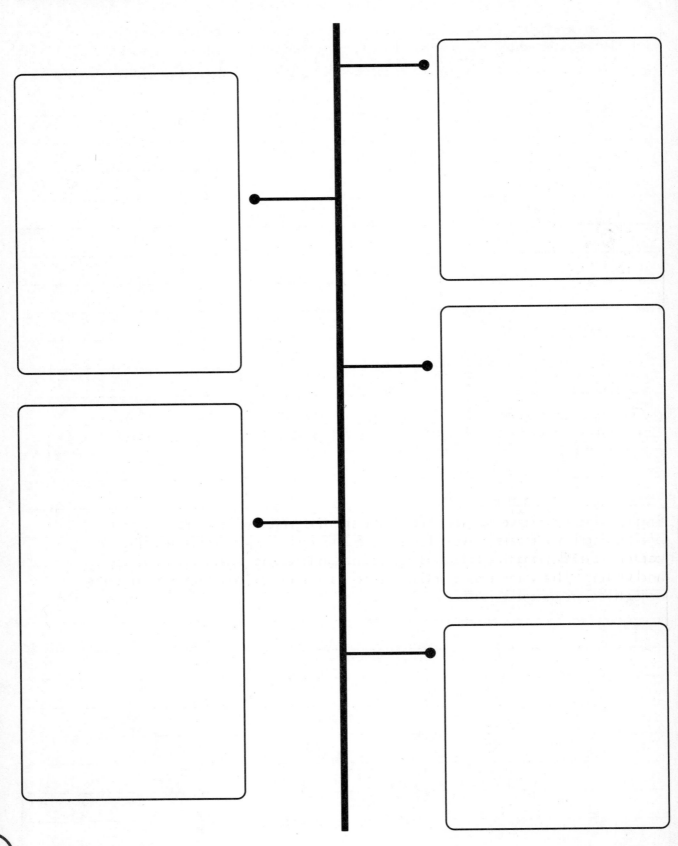